NEWSWIRE

NEWSWIRE

SEENI

authorHOUSE®

AuthorHouse™
1663 Liberty Drive
Bloomington, IN 47403
www.authorhouse.com
Phone: 1-800-839-8640

© 2012 by SEENI. All rights reserved.

No part of this book may be reproduced, stored in a retrieval system, or transmitted by any means without the written permission of the author.

Published by AuthorHouse   04/04/2012

ISBN: 978-1-4678-9711-2 (sc)
ISBN: 978-1-4678-9712-9 (e)

All images within the interior of the book have been photograph by the author.

Because of the dynamic nature of the Internet, any web addresses or links contained in this book may have changed since publication and may no longer be valid. The views expressed in this work are solely those of the author and do not necessarily reflect the views of the publisher, and the publisher hereby disclaims any responsibility for them.

Dedication

For Brenda Lavender

Contents

Dedication Page i
Contents iii

Chapter 1 1
Chapter 2 17
Chapter 3 25
Chapter 4 31
Chapter 5 39
Chapter 6 43
Chapter 7 48
Chapter 8 54
Chapter 9 57
Chapter 10 62
Chapter 11 67

Acknowledgements iv
About the Author v

Chapter 1

Damian Sinclair and Klara Klaber met each other, on the first day of enrolment at the University of Lancaster in Lancashire. It was a cold breezy day in October 1973 when their eyes met for the first time. Both thought that there was something special in each other. Damian enrolled for an Honours Degree in Geography and Klara enrolled for an Honours Degree in Botany in the faculty of science.

Damian was the only child of John and Joan Sinclair who had his upbringing in Preston Lancashire. Klara was one of three daughters of Joseph and Maria Klaber who were of Hungarian descent. They lived in Chipping in Lancashire. The middle class values and attitudes of both families allowed them to have high aspirations.

As the days and months went by they got to know each other and enjoyed each other's company. Both Simon and Klara talked about each other to their families and visited them during their vacations. Both enjoyed their studies and worked very hard to obtain good grades in their respective subjects. At the beginning of their third year at university, they left their halls of residence and moved into a self-contained student flat close to the university. Here they had a certain degree of privacy and a closeness which they enjoyed. Damian and Klara had fallen in love with each other. The parents of both were happy and gave their support. Klara's older sister Zia and younger sister Simoni however, were slightly concerned that they were too quick with their decisions.

Damian had enjoyed travelling before he met Klara. He often discussed with Klara that he would like to travel to Africa with her. There was so much excitement in his voice when he spoke about the Continent. One day, he put it to her "would you join me to have a year off after graduation?" Klara's eyes lit up. She said "that would be good. Is that a promise?" There was so much excitement in her voice too. Damian replied "most certainly" During her younger days she had travelled with her sisters Zia and Simoni to Europe and had much fun.

After having worked very hard at university they completed their studies in July 1977. On graduation day they both obtained upper second Degrees. Both families were very pleased and they took pride in their children's achievements. Both researched the parts of Africa they wished to travel and perhaps work. Before they travelled Damian was successful in finding a temporary job as a clerk in the Planning Department at Lancaster City Hall and Klara started work as a Library Assistant at the University of Lancaster. They saved as much money as they possibly could, but the parents of both helped them generously.

In December 1977, the year of Queen Elizabeth's Silver Jubilee Damian and Klara followed a meticulous plan and approach towards their itinerary. They flew on a British Airways flight from Manchester via London to Johannesburg and from there to Harare in Zimbabwe on a South African Airways flight. The flight time took its toll and they were very tired but enjoyed the flight.

A long taxi ride from the airport took them to their destination-The Victoria Falls Hotel. As they drove close to the hotel they saw the Victoria Bridge which looked Majestic. Klara said "I cannot believe I am here." Damian replied "one has to thank the British for this masterpiece." As the taxi stopped near the reception area of the hotel, the beautifully clad concierge in a white colonial suit welcomed them. He said "good afternoon Madam and Sir, my name is Thomas. If you need my services please call me on 222." He escorted them to suite 1002. They were amazed at the British influence in the décor and style of the bedroom. The view of the Victoria Bridge from the bedroom was awesome. Damian and Klara were ecstatic, that they immediately called their family on their mobile phones. Klara said "mum you must see this to believe. The hotel and the bridge are out of this world." Damian said "we reached safely. I will call you on another day."

A new look-out point below the terrace looking directly on the Victoria Falls Bridge and the Botoka Gorge, are classic additions to the landscaped garden. The evenings however brought in the mosquitoes. Damian and Klara used the anti-mosquito sprays and creams diligently although they took a course of anti-malarial tablets. They saw the gardens growing and the frogs in the ponds who must know that the rains will soon be here. Their evening chorus beckons them on. Klara picked mangoes from the trees in the courtyard which gave off a unique fragrance. On one of the evenings they took a ride on the original boat ride along the Zambesi River. With sightings of Crocodiles in the muddy river this was truly and adventure.

Victoria Bridge and Falls

As the days got warm Damian and Klara enjoyed the air-conditioned Livingstone dining room. Guests are requested to be formally dressed for dinner to keep up with the past colonial traditions. At lunch time the coolest place to have a light lunch is the "Jungle Junction." Built in the style of a summer house the Jungle Junction's high thatched roof, fans and the granolithic floor made it most comfortable on even the hottest days. Klara and Damian enjoyed the lemonade made from the lemons grown in the gardens of this hotel. They spent many hours in the hotel shop to explore old photographs, railway souvenirs and items that could only be found in this hotel. Five days at this magnificent place was indeed memorable.

They learned that the Victoria Falls had existed for millions of years, but it was not until David Livingstone visited in 1855 that the outside world came to know of the cataracts. It is believed that the development of the Victoria Falls as a world renowned tourist attraction, started only with the arrival of the railway heading north to Cairo in 1904. In May 1904 the railway company quickly despatched the materials for the construction of the first Victoria Falls Hotel. As years passed by and the hotel moved into the millennium, it was ready to host more generations of guests wishing to combine a visit to the greatest natural wonder of southern Africa—The Victoria falls. From the beginning Klara and Damian made notes of their visits and used their tape recorder and microphone where possible.

Damian and Klara spent their last evening at the hotel, dining in the famous Livingstone dining room. The brass band played on. This added to the nostalgia of the gracious room. They were attended by their personal waiter known as Boso. Damian ordered Champagne and Boso poured it into Damian's glass. Damian nodded to Boso and he poured the Champagne into both their glasses. To Klara's surprise Damian opened a small silver jewellery box which contained the most beautiful diamond and ruby engagement ring. Klara was uneasy and she blushed. Damian gently held her left hand and placed it on her finger. Then as if rehearsed they both said "I love you" to each other simultaneously. Damian moved from his chair and went towards Klara and kissed her full red lips.

They enjoyed the eight course meal. After a while the headwaiter brought a little cake with one candle which was lit. The rest of the waiters clapped when Klara blew the candle. Klara was ecstatic. It showed on her beautiful face. They later danced cheek to cheek to the music of the live band. Klara whispered in Damian's ear "this is the best day of my life." At 02.00hrs they went to bed feeling quite exhausted but happy.

At around 05.00 hrs Damian was woken up by the ringing of the hotel telephone. He took the receiver in his hand and said "hello." It was the telephone operator who said "Sir, there is a call for you from England." Damian thought this must be bad news and we have only just started our journey. He then heard his dad's voice who said "Damian you have come up on the lottery" Damian said "How much?" His father said "a large sum. I will call you again." Damian got back into bed, and hugged Klara and said "We have won a lot of money. It was dad on the telephone." Klara looked dazed. They could not get back to sleep.

Damian and Klara had their showers, got dressed and went for early breakfast before their departure for Johannesburg. On the way to the dining room they had to pass the reception. The telephone operator said "good morning madam, good morning Sir" congratulations for winning the lottery." Klara and Damian were horrified that the operator had listened to the telephone conversation. They both were very unhappy about this but carried on with breakfast. They were glad to leave soon. At around 10.00hrs they left the Victoria Falls hotel for Harare airport to continue their journey to Johannesburg. From here they had to take a taxi to Pretoria. At the airport they hired a taxi driven by Joseph. He did speak good English. He asked Damian "did you come from England?" "He naively answered "No, we just arrived from the Victoria hotel Zimbabwe and we will travel to Cape Town." Just then Joseph said my relatives work in Zimbabwe and Cape Town."

On their way to Pretoria, Joseph explained that Pretoria is known as the Jacaranda city on account of the thousand Jacaranda trees which lined the wide city streets. The city had much to do with Marthinus Wessels Pretorius, son of the original Voortrekkers, Andries Pretorius. Joseph seemed very knowledgeable. He informed that the city and its environment allowed the interaction and progress of the Afrikaans people with other cultures. There were two structures which dominated Pretoria skyline. The union building designed by Sir Herbert Baker, to serve as the government's administration headquarters and the Voortrekker monument, a massive granite shrine commemorating the Voortrekkers.

Damian and Klara held hands and were attentively listening to Joseph's commentary. They also taped this commentary. Joseph showed the city's fine railway station as another of the many imposing buildings in South Africa designed by Sir Herbert Baker, co-designer of the city of New Delhi in India. Joseph said that the railway was commissioned in 1920 some fifty one years before South Africa was proclaimed a Republic.

Seeni

Victoria Falls

At the end of the taxi ride Joseph drove onto the entrance of the gracious old Victoria hotel Pretoria on the corner of Scheidung street and Paul Kruger (formerly Market street). It serves as the headquarters of Rovos Rail and boasts a five star standard. This magnificent old hotel was originally built in 1892 by a Mr Hambourg who called it the Station Hotel. Damian and Klara were informed that a Mr Jacob Joffe took over the business and rebuilt it in 1896 and named it the Hollandia Hotel. But only four years later whilst Lord Robert and his British troops occupied Pretoria, the Hollandia was renamed Victoria.

Damian and Klara learned that a Mr Ros and his team have painstakingly restored this majestic hotel to its original glory, revealing the elegance and charm of the bygone era. The hotel now offers a very cosy fireside pub with the theme of the train depicted on a huge mural painting. The restaurant with its fountain and palm trees creates the wonderful ambience reminiscent of the 1920's. Highly qualified staff members await your every wish. The hotel has a conference room catering for eighty people.

Having observed the front of the hotel Damian and Klara checked into their bedroom, which was one of ten beautifully appointed rooms with en-suite bathrooms and toilet facilities. Both were pleasantly surprised at this luxurious place and the courteous, interested and focused staff.

Having received their luggage in the bedroom, the concierge handed a letter addressed to Damian. The letter took him by surprise. They both thought it was a welcome letter from the manager. He quickly opened it and to his astonishment read what follows. "Congratulations. Enjoy your time in South Africa." There was no sender's name. Damian and Klara looked at each other in dismay. Damian locked the bedroom door and took a call to his dad from his roaming mobile phone. "Dad, he said, I am worried" His dad said "What is worrying you?" Damian said "There are people here who are aware of the lottery winning. First it was in Zimbabwe and now here at the hotel" Damian's dad replied "I am so sorry Son, I should not have phoned you on the land line." Damian said "Please don't call us on land line phones. We will call you." They said their goodbyes and Damian switched off his phone. Klara was distressed, it showed on her face. However they had their showers and rested for a couple of hours.

At around 17.30 hrs Damian and Klara got dressed up and went downstairs for a drink at the hotel Pub. There they met a few passengers who would join them in the most luxurious train in the world—The "Rovos Rail." About half an hour later they were ready for dinner which consisted of a four course meal. The delicious and sumptuous meal was enjoyed by all.

The following morning was spent exploring the Victoria Hotel Pretoria. After lunch they organised themselves for departure at 16.45 hrs to the private railway terminal at Capital Park. On arrival Damian and Klara were inducted into the golden age of luxury train travel which has been renewed in the heart of the African Bush. This beautifully restored train consisted of twenty coaches that could be drawn either by steam, diesel or electricity. The sleepers, the observation and dining cars have been splendidly refurbished in the style of the period but with an eye for modern comfort. The train carries a maximum of seventy two passengers who are attended by personal staff who are highly skilled and well motivated. The cuisine is of a superb standard befitting an exclusive form.

Initially there was the welcome information which consisted of security items such as opening and closing shutters and windows, the operation of the air-conditioning unit, fire extinguishers, gas geysers and the bar refrigerator. They were also inducted into room service, laundry service, maps, itineraries, the make up of the train, the gift shop, off-train excursions, and the most important item the passports.

Damian and Klara were welcomed by their personal hostess Julia and she directed them to the cabin/suite 8104. They were requested to unpack and freshen up in their suite, prior to joining the other passengers in the observation carriage at the rear of the train. This allowed the exchange of formalities with the others. Both Damian and Klara exchanged greetings with a few of the passengers. They however had more time with Hans-Peter, Helmut, Brenda, Kielan and Agi. Later Klara whispered to Damian "what a splendid experience" Damian then hugged and kissed her in affirmation of her remark. They showed great excitement and looked forward to the train journey. A glass of champagne was served for each person. Mr Ros, the Head of "The Rovos Rail" had a word with every passenger. He informed all that the locomotives would be exchanged in 5 minutes at Germistan. We would then depart for Johannesburg which was 70 km away. Last of all Mr Ros reminded the passengers that dinner was served at 19.30 hrs and the need for formal attire. The passengers however expected this formality and the code of ethics as written in the brochures.

At around 19.15 hrs Damian and Klara were dressed and made their way to the dining car to be greeted by Sylvester who would be their personal waiter.

He then directed them to their seats for the meal, handed the ala-carte menu and the wine list which consisted of South Africa's best. This was a great experience for Damian and Klara. The food was sumptuous and the wine went down nicely with the meal. On finishing their dinner Damian and Klara went into their cabins around 23.00 hrs. To their surprise they found the bed was decorated with sprigs of Bougainvillea flowers. A box of chocolate was placed on one pillow with a card saying "Good night, sweet dreams." They were both ecstatic. Damian said "I am so glad we came." Klara said "if my sisters saw me now." The most interesting features were the bath and shower. To have a bath while the train moved was such a unique experience.

Leaving Pretoria the "Pride of Africa" (the name given to this train) moved gently as it moved eastwards towards Kempton Park, a dormitory city adjacent to Johannesburg, the largest city in the sub-Saharan Africa. It is on the heights of the Witwatersrand some 1828 meters (6000ft) above sea level, that the greatest goldfields in history were discovered before the turn of the century.

Damian and Klara were keen to learn the geographical, historical, social and economical aspects of this vast country as they travelled. They were both hungry for general points of interest on the journey. They learned that prior to 1886, maps of the area where Johannesburg now stands, depicted only a series of bush covered ridges from which flowed a few small streams. When gold was discovered on the Witwatersrand, a vibrant tent-town grew rapidly into a frontier city and then into a dynamic commercial and financial centre, now the capital of the Gauteng region. (Until recently this region was known as PWV, meaning Pretoria-Witswatersrand-Vereeniging).

The passengers learned that Gauteng is the smallest and the richest of the mine regions formed in terms of South Africa's interim constitution of the 27th April 1994. The name is sotho. It is a tribal, verbal corruption of the Afrikaans word "goud" which means gold. The gold bearing main reef was first struck by a man named George Harrison, when he stumbled across an outcrop edging above the surface of the land. It is believed that this spot can be viewed in a park four kilometres west of the city centre where sandy quartz which trapped the fine gold dust around 2700 million years ago is still clearly visible.

The hostess Julia explained to Damian and Klara, that the gigantic forces of nature were once responsible for producing the gold metal so precious to South Africa's economy today. She stated that the volcanic rock was scoured and eroded away over hundreds of millions of years by water. It is believed that gold was released from igneous rock which had washed southwards to be held for an eternity in a series of fossilised beaches allowing it to subside. Many years later man arrived into one of natures greatest wonders—the supply of gold, a lustrous, highly valued commodity held in vast quantities by the major nations of the world.

Reading the maps and other literature Klara and Damian learned that from the early days of 1886, the Witwatersrand gold fields stretched along a gentle curve 120km (72miles) from Benom to Krugersdorf. This was unique. It is believed that the amount of gold in the ore is low, but the tidal reservoir of gold bearing ore appears to be limitless. These two factors have determined the profile of the gold mining industry in Africa. No single person could manage the industry. Only one mining house consisting of several shareholders were able to raise the imposing capital, needed to successfully mine and process the enormous quantities of ore from which small quantities of gold are finally extracted.

Damian and Klara spent time in the "Pride of Africa's library" and with the well informed members of staff who were eager that we were exposed to this vast country. It would appear that the mine dumps of Gauteng are disappearing, as they are reprocessed using advanced technology to capture small quantities of gold, which escaped in the less refined methods of past years. Damian and Klara were informed that the world's deepest mines 4.7km (3mls) below the surface of the earth are found in South Africa.

Milling of the ore was only half the equation. The other half is the extraction of the ore. Using cheap labour provided by large numbers of able bodied men enabled the extraction. Yet despite the small size, the mining houses acted as entrepreneurs, identified new prospects to carry out exhaustive feasibility studies and keep the economy of the country stable. Julia believed that South Africa owes its state of development to gold. Over six hundred tons of the precious metal which were produced every year by the mining houses, have paved the way, directly or indirectly for the industrialisation and modernisation of a traditional South African society. Today with a democratic government in place South Africa has taken up its rightful role as the powerhouse of the African Continent.

Damian and Klara listened to the gems of knowledge and experienced sensory overload. However they continued to discuss their travel so far, with each other before they slept in this comfortable cabin. At 06.00 hrs they were woken up by Julia. Breakfast was served at 08.00 hrs. and they were ready for it.

The "Pride of Africa" left the golden city heading towards the Vaal River, which marks the boundary between the Transvaal and the Orange Free State. They passed through Bloemhof and Leeudoringstand en-route for Kimberley 493 Km from Johannesburg. In Kimberley the "Pride of Africa" enters one of the finest Victorian railway stations in Africa. A product of the railway's hey day of the 1810's. The cast iron girders encased in glass soared over the platforms to recall the intricate patterns of a bygone era.

Damian and Klara along with the rest of the passengers disembarked the train and proceeded to the waiting coach for a tour of the city, the "Big Hole", the mining museum and a ride through the city on a historic tram.

During the tour Damian and Klara had the opportunity to socialise with some of the other passengers. Helmut and Hans-Peter who were from Germany discussed their views so far. Aggi who came from Iceland was quite amusing and Klara enjoyed his wit. Just then one of the staff came to join this group. He introduced himself as Bob. He asked if we are finding the trip enjoyable. Damian said that it is out of this world and they were impressed. Bob was a very hearty and a burly character. He turned towards Damian in the presence of the rest in the group and said "A little bird told me of your good news sir, congratulations for winning the lottery." Damian replied immediately and remarked. "It's a scam, don't believe everything you here." He was angry inside but did not show it. What seemed a very enjoyable day turned out to be a rather anxious one. Klara remained calm and did not contribute to the question that was asked. During the trip Damian spoke to his dad again and said "there is "a newswire" and there are more people who know about it." Damian's dad once again was apologetic. He said "I am so sorry I ever called you, but I did because you wanted me to before you started the journey."

The Big Hole-Kimberley

On the guided tour Patrick the guide explained to the passengers that the discovery of gold on the Witwatersrand in 1886 and the consolidation of the diamond industry by Rhodes and De Beers in 1888 allowed wealth to ebb from Kimberley never to return. It is however a charming town preserved and unchanged in many ways over the years, owing to the presence of De Beers, the world's largest specialist diamond dealing company. Kimberley was among those South African towns besieged by the Boers during the Anglo-Boer war. All this was very interesting but for Damian and Klara, the issue about the "newswire" was turning into a distraction which they never wanted. It spoiled the day for them.

The tour continued by the group visiting the diamond museum, an intensely interesting and carefully constructed display of historical memorabilia housed next to the "Big Hole", the largest man-made excavation in the world. This astonishing excavation was once the site of a small hill on which diamondiferous "blue ground" Kimberlite was discovered. Would—be miners from all corners of the globe sought to make fortunes here. Tons of ore were removed as the diggers continued their search, hundreds of feet below ground level. Damian and Klara had plenty of time to take photographs of this fascinating place.

It is believed that very few of those early diggers had any idea about how diamonds came into being. The group was told that diamonds were created about fifty three million years ago, some 200 km beneath the surface under conditions of unimaginable heat and pressure. Patrick explained that carbon was changed into diamond, the hardest substance known to man.

After a very informative morning they returned to the train around 13.00hrs in time for lunch that was enjoyed by all. Damian and Klara returned to their suite, checked their belongings, had their showers and had a rest in their cabin. They did not speak much but they new in their hearts that the "newswire" is always on their minds and they were unable to control or stop it.

Leaving the diamond city the "Pride of Africa" continued its journey southwards towards De-Aar, a major railway junction to Namibia and the Northern Cape line. The changing vegetation provided the passengers with an indication of the increasingly arid nature of the region as the train headed southwards into the heart of the Karoo 1220m (4000ft) high. Damian and Klara learned that this region offered solace to Victorian sufferers of Tuberculosis. Julia's information revealed that this was an enormous inland sea. Over millions of years volcanic matter was ground down and deposited as silt upon the sea bed to form what geologists call the Karoo system.

The train was now speeding its way along the great central spine of Africa, which stretches all the way to Ethiopia at an average height of around 1200m (400ft) above sea level. The edge of the escarpment is always more dramatic on the east side of the train than on the west side.

The vast herds of Springboks (Antidoreas Marsupialis) of one hundred and fifty years ago have been replaced by sheep, one of the few animals able to survive on the low lying shrubs. That is the common vegetation in Karoo. Springboks once migrated across the Karoo in herds of about 40,000—A sight once viewed by David Livingstone, but no more.

A sleepy village, a few hours travel south of De Aar was Victoria West. It was once a thriving centre used as a re-fuelling stop for flights from London to Cape Town taking ten days, with a flying time limited to day-light hours in the 1940's. This was of particular interest to Damian and Klara.

Leaving Victoria West the "Pride of Africa" headed south for the "Three sisters," a trio of buttes or rounded and eroded hillocks well known to travellers in South Africa. Travelling further south the train passed through Beaufort-West, a town founded in 1818 by the Governor of the Cape, Lord Charles Somerset and named this place after his father, the Duke of Beaufort.

At around 08.25 hrs travelling 738Km from Kimberley, the train arrived at Matjiesfontein and breakfast was served. After breakfast the passengers disembarked from the train. They stepped into this historic city of over hundred years ago. Laird Logan set up a small refreshment hotel for the hungry and thirsty travellers of the Cape government railway. This authentic railway village stands perfectly preserved. Legend has it, that an occasional visit from the ghost of a wounded British "Tommy" of the Anglo-Boer war is seen.

The graceful old hotel is named after the much maligned British imperialist, Lord Milner under Lord Cromer, the British Agent in Cairo. Damian and Klara were keen to learn the historical aspects and the British influence in this country. Anton the guide was eager to describe it in English. It appeared that Lord Milner was appointed High Commissioner for South Africa by the then British Colonial Secretary Joe Chamberlain in 1898. He had insisted that Paul Kruger, the President of the old Transvaal Republic extend the franchise to include the "uitlanders" (The Afrikaans term for foreigner).He had said "they were after all paying taxes and had lived for twelve years in the Transvaal." Kruger had flatly refused to share his Republic with others, an attitude that led to the declaration of the

Anglo-Boer war in 1899. Anton made history very interesting for Damian and Klara. Before returning to the train Damian and Klara strolled through the quaint village observing the old post office, the Lairds Arms a Victorian country pub, the old museum suite and the coffee house. They allowed themselves to live in this historic settlement for just a little while.

At around 11.00 hrs the train left Matjiesfontein and travelled southwards towards Touws River, leaving behind the strangely haunting barren land of the great Karoo, as it descended to the first terraces and the vineyards of the Hex river valley. Damian and Klara held hands and watched the fine old cape Dutch houses dotted among the patchwork of the vineyards. They were fascinated by the scenery and were reminded of the early settlers who came from Holland, when they saw the quaint Amsterdam town houses dotted around the land and the snow mountain surrounding the valley. The train then continued to lose altitude, reaching the first mountain terrace and the town Worcester before heading for Paarl in the heart of the vinelands.

Close to Cape Town the vegetation was tinged green by the winter rain of the Western Cape, a region which enjoys a Mediterranean climate. They were informed that in the long hot summers the vegetation turned a burnt brown hue. In winter the vines shed their autumn leaves bearing their gnarled limbs. As spring had moved into early summer the vineyards appeared richly covered in fruit. They believed that some of the best wine in the world is made from the grapes harvested from those prolific vineyards. Damian and Klara had the opportunity to taste some of this wine in the "pride of Africa".

The three day/two night rail journey was sadly coming to an end for Damian and Klara. They saw Cape Town, which is internationally known for the majestic Table Mountain. This is the mother city of South Africa—the site of the first European landing and settlement. The arrival of the first Europeans at the foot of Africa had met with little resistance from the Cape's only human inhabitants—the Hottentots. Black tribes were encountered for the first time by eastward migrating white farmers after 1702, about 700km (420ml) east of Cape Town around the Great Fish River—a meeting of two divergent cultures the consequences of which are still unfolding today.

Seeni

Damian and Klara experienced extravagant elegance of rail travel on one of the most luxurious trains in the world-The Rovos Rail's unique steam safaris through the heart of Africa. The combination of some of the most magnificent scenery with the glamour and excitement of the golden age of steam, the beautifully restored train offered accommodation of the highest standard, combining the opulence of pre-war travel with subtle modern innovations. They were ecstatic at their experience but soon they will leave.

Chapter 2

At Cape Town railway station, the Rovos Rail staff sorted the luggage and put these into a hailed taxi. Damian and Klara got in and requested the taxi driver Ben to take them to the pre-booked Cape Grace Hotel near the waterfront marina and the west quay. On the way to the hotel Ben informed them that the history of the Victoria and Alfred waterfront dates back to 1860, when Prince Alfred who was Queen Victoria's second son tipped fine rock for construction on Cape Town's original breakwater. The original Alfred Basin could not handle the increase shipping volume brought by the advent of steam and subsequently a large basin, the Victoria basin was built.

Damian and Klara hoped to stay in Cape Town for five days. After which the itinerary would take them through the "Garden Route." They were glad that the train journey was behind them and another section of their journey would begin. During their stay in Cape Town they had a look around the city. Particular areas which interested them were the clock tower built in 1883, the synchrolift, the seal landing, the maritime museum, the waterfront craft market. One that caught their interest was Robben Island. The Hildebrand restaurant was visited many times. The BMW pavilion Imax Cinema is the only one in Africa that has a giant screen five storeys high, with 15.000 watts of six channel wrap-around digital sound to create a larger than life experience. The result was breathtaking images of unsurpassed size and impact—in essence one has to see this Imax experience to believe.

A ride on the cableway of the Table Mountain was not to be missed. A group tour arranged by the hotel allowed Damian and Klara to do just that. The cableway took them from the lower cable station on Tafelberg road about 302m above sea level to the plateau at the top of the mountain. The cable car rotated through 350 degrees during the ascent and descent giving a panoramic view over the city. The Table Mountain is a flat topped mountain forming a prominent landmark overlooking the city of Cape Town, and is featured on the flag of Cape Town. The mountain forms part of the Table Mountain national park. The elevation is 1,084.6 m (3,558ft). The composition of the rock is a type of sandstone. Damian and Klara conversed with a few of the tourists and had one of the most exhilarating experiences so far.

On their return to the hotel, Damian was given a message by the receptionist. It was a typed written note requesting Damian to meet with Joseph the taxi driver who drove them to the hotel in Pretoria. Damian was asked to give him a telephone call. Klara remarked "I wonder what he wants" Damian said "the best way to get to know is to call him." He then made a call to the number typed on the message. Joseph responded "good evening Sir, I hope you didn't mind me calling you, but my brother Philip is in Cape Town. He is a reliable driver. You did say that you may take the "Garden Route," so I wondered if you would arrange with him to take you down. His price is good." Klara listened to the conversation. Initially she was happy but her face fell. She thought, "How did Joseph know the hotel we were in?" Damian said, "I am not going to call Philip." Klara said, "Every time we go out there is a message, it is very spooky." Damian said "don't worry we are not in England now, this is a different world." They had their showers and were getting ready for dinner, when the telephone rang. Klara answered the call. It was Philip asking for Damian. Klara said "please hold on for a moment." She called out for Damian who was in the bathroom and said "it is Philip." Damian came to the telephone, and said "ah, you are Joseph's brother, he informed us about you. "Could you give us a moment?" Damian said to Klara, "there is no harm him talking to us in the hotel, we should ask him to come to the hotel" Klara said "ok then." Damian spoke to Philip "you could come to the hotel reception in an hour."

Damian and Klara freshened up and got dressed for dinner. They came down to the foyer / reception area to be greeted by Philip. He was well dressed in a white suit. He introduced himself and shook hands with both of them. Philip handed them a package of route maps and hotels in the 'Garden Route'. He also showed them three references one of which was the hotel they were at. Philip said "I am a registered driver for this hotel."

At this Damian and Klara were at ease. Damian said "we will study all this and give you a call when we set the date." They said their goodbyes. Damian and Klara checked with the hotel if Philip was actually registered with them. They affirmed that Philip was reliable and they often called on him for tourists.

Dinner at the hotel restaurant allowed Damian and Klara to relax and discuss important issues. Damian whispered to Klara "I must talk with the Euro-Million management although dad has already spoken on my behalf" Klara replied "you really must talk to dad before long" After dinner Klara used her mobile phone to talk with her family. Klara's mother said to her "you sound tense, is every thing alright?" Klara said "we are tired otherwise things seemed to go on well." Coffee was served in the veranda when two Englishman entered the area and asked "you don't mind if we join you?" Damian replied "please join us." One of them was called Jason and the other Julian who came from Bristol. They were architects. During the course of the conversation, Damian described the Rovos Rail journey to them and they did envy the experience. Julian asked Klara "where do you intend to travel next?" She was cautious about saying much to strangers. She replied "we hope to travel east." Jason described some of the places they had visited. It turned out to be a joyous evening.

During the next day they gave much thought about hiring Philip. After much discussion they decided to call him to establish the itinerary which included the night stops on the "Garden Route." Philip turned up in the evening as he was already escorting other tourists during the day. At face value Philip seemed to be a very professional driver. They arranged the formalities and the price. Both Damian and Klara felt comfortable with him.

On the following day Damian and Klara having packed their luggage checked out from the hotel. Philip was prompt. He turned up in a white Toyota People Carrier and placed the travel bags in the vehicle. This was followed by them receiving a travel document package. Philip discussed the route briefly. Damian and Klara made themselves comfortable and the journey commenced at around 08.30 hrs. It was a beautiful day, the sun shone against a clear blue sky. The temperature was 28º C.

On day one they travelled towards the historic oak lined town of Stellenbosch. This is a town in the Western Cape Province, situated 55 km from Cape Town on the banks of the Erste River on the hilly region of the Cape vinelands. The vehicle came to a stop and Philip opened the car doors, Damian and Klara were introduced to wine tasting and a visit to the historic city. The amazing sight of the white buildings was truly awesome. The village museum was well worth a visit however, time was limited on this occasion. Philip informed them that Stellenbosch University was one of the South Africa's leading universities. The wine tasting got Klara somewhat light headed, she could not stop giggling. The route took its course onto Franschoek for lunch. They were hungry and ready for the meal which they enjoyed. Philip showed great care while driving. Damian and Klara felt less apprehensive as South Africa is noted for reckless drivers resulting in major road traffic accidents. Frequent notices along the roadside displayed the number of accidents for a particular month. This scared both Klara and Damian.

The "Garden Route" continued in the afternoon to Grabouw and Elgin which were the apple growing regions, before arriving at the coastal haven of Kleinmond. They checked in at the pre-booked Beach House Hotel for dinner and overnight accommodation. This was a quaint hotel overlooking the beach. This hotel has stood overlooking Sandown Bay for decades and has become a landmark for travellers and holiday makers.

After settling down in their bedroom Damian, Klara and Philip walked along the wide sea beach prior to dinner being served. The hospitality afforded by the landlord Louis and his wife Karina was unique and special.

On the second day of their tour Philip drove Damian and Klara from Kleinmond to Swellendam, over the Tradouwe Pass to Calitzdorf and Outschoorn. A visit to Highgate Ostrich, crocodile and Cheetah farm was an experience, especially when lunch included Ostrich meat which was not enjoyed by them, after having seen the live gracious animals earlier.

The tour continued in the afternoon passing over the Robinson Pass. This was very scenic and Damian continued to take photographs at every opportunity. Dinner and overnight stay was at King George 111, a luxury accommodation situated in the heart of the "Garden Route" overlooking a golf course with a view of the Outeniqua Mountains. Philip was quiet throughout except when he accepted several mobile telephone calls. This made Klara nervous. She seemed suspicious of Philip. Damian and Klara relaxed in the swimming pool and had time to talk to their families. Klara said "mum, you will be envious if you saw this place." Damian had a few minutes with his parents too. They had time to discuss the trip and write their notes prior to dinner which was enjoyed by both Damian and Klara. After a restful night and a sumptuous breakfast they looked for the next section of the "Garden Route."

On day three they continued travelling towards George when Damian and Klara stepped on board the well known Outeniqua "Choo-Choo," a unique train ride to Kynsa. Meanwhile Philip had pre-booked a check-in at the Country Crescent hotel situated in Plettenberg bay with dinner and overnight accommodation. Plettenberg bay nestles in one of the most beautiful settings on the "Garden Route" There were long white sandy beaches against a backdrop of stately Blue Mountains. It offered something for all from nature lovers to the sporting enthusiast.

The last day of the "Garden Route" was worth waiting for. Damian and Klara could not believe that such a place existed. Instantly they both fell in love with it. Philip said it was his favourite place in South Africa. It was none other than the Tsitsikamma coastal national park. Philip explained that in 1964 it was proclaimed as the first coastal national park on the African continent. This sanctuary in the southern Cape covers an area of marine life some 100km long, between the Groot (big) river, the mouth is near Humansdorf to the east and to a point near the celebrated Plettenberg bay resort area to the west. The park consisted not only the shore-line and 5 km of water out to sea, but also landwards of a narrow coastal plain with its marginal cliffs, so sheer and massive that they screen the rocky shores and its isolated beaches from the interior and the Tsitsikamma mountains to the north. It is here that rivers cut their way through gorges to the sea. Looking out they saw streams and natural pools everywhere. The water was soft brown to amber caused neither by dirt nor pollution but owing to organic acids from vegetable matter. The 8km long tarred road on which Philip drove and the scenic highway ran inwards almost parallel with the coast.

Philip stopped the vehicle in the parking area of the forest. There they bought tea and cake and continued to enjoy the fascinating place. They had the opportunity to meet Jason the manager. He explained "the Tsitsikamma Forests is managed by the Department of water Affaires and Forestry Commission of South Africa." Damian and Klara discussed with him work opportunities for foreigners in this area. Klara explained to him of their qualifications and interest. Jason replied "Here's my card. May be you could call and we could discuss further." Damian explained that they would be spending a few days in Port Elizabeth. They were both comfortable with Jason. Klara said "I like his openness and attitude." Damian said "He is a rare gem."

Philip came over and collected Damian and Klara to the vehicle. It was early evening and the 'Garden Route' ends at Port Elizabeth. Philip was in pensive thought and did not speak with either of them. He said "I have another tourist trip this evening." There was not much conversation. At around 20.00 hrs they reached Port Elizabeth and checked in at the pre-booked hotel, the Nurberg Mountain Inn for one nights accommodation. This hotel was about one hours travelling distance from the centre of Port Elizabeth. It was in yet another spectacular mountain setting on the popular Addo national park. Philip carried the luggage into the hotel. Both Damian and Klara thanked him for his care in driving. Before he left Damian handed a fifty sterling pound note for himself as a gratuity. Philip did not look happy and said "I thought that I could expect more from someone who had a lottery winning." At this Damian said "you must not believe rumours we have worked hard to make this trip." Philip replied "don't ask me how I know, but you cannot keep good fortune a secret." Having said these words he got into his vehicle and drove on. Damian and Klara entered their very comfortable bedroom and lay on the beds for a while. Klara said "He was so quiet all day. I knew something was up. He had several telephone calls too." He kept it till the last to talk about the lottery winning." Damian said "If only dad had given thought before he called on the landline. Why did he not use my mobile number?" Klara replied "I am really scared may be we should return to England" Damian said "Lets freshen up and have dinner first. I am hungry."

Tsitsikamma

After dinner which was enjoyed by both, they spoke with their families. Damian's dad asked them to return, but Klara's family were not overly concerned about what they discussed. After a good night's sleep in this cosy hotel they had breakfast and made their way to the Addo national park to view the 220 herd of Elephants. It was very close to their hotel. There were many tourist buses and other vehicles. The Elephants looked so majestic and almost enjoyed the visitors.

They returned in the early hours of the evening and booked another night in this superb hotel as it was too late to find another for the rest of their days in central Port Elizabeth.

They mingled with a few guests after dinner and discussed the Addo national park and its wonderful Elephants. Later Klara and Damian spent the evening sunshine reminiscing the days in South Africa, writing their notes and viewing the photographs in their digital camera.

Damian whispered to Klara "I am so glad that I made this journey with you." In the years to come we will have such happy memories and we will then be able to tell our children. Klara, hugged Damian and said "I am so very happy, I wish these feelings will last for ever and ever."

Prior to settling down for the night both Klara and Damian called the respective families, who seemed delighted once again to hear their voices. Klara's sisters in particular were very excited about their great opportunity.

Before they went to sleep it was necessary for them to pack all their belongings in readiness for their departure from this most comfortable accommodation close to the Addo National Park.

Chapter 3

Damian and Klara spent another night in this luxurious accommodation. In the morning they hired a hotel taxi and dropped themselves in the centre of Port Elizabeth by the tourist information centre. They found the staff very helpful. After careful scrutiny they booked themselves at the Bay Lodge Guest House for three nights. This was a quality accommodation in central Port Elizabeth. The owner/managers were called Janet and Keith, an English couple originally from Cornwall. They made Damian and Klara feel warm and comfortable. Klara commented "I do hope Philip does not know of our whereabouts." Damian replied "don't be too sure of that, the newswire is still active."

After a good night's sleep and a tasty English breakfast they walked the streets of the city. They learned that Port Elizabeth is known as the "friendly city." It is the main gateway to the Eastern Cape and is the biggest coastal city between Cape Town and Durban. It is believed to be a year round holiday resort and a major commercial/industrial city with fine shops, restaurants, sporting facilities and very old library. Port Elizabeth overlooks splendid beaches and warm blue waters of the Algoa bay and the Jackass colony. It is a Mecca for sailing, swimming, surfing, diving and all other water sports.

During the three days here, they spent some time in the provincial legislative buildings and East London. This is a bustling and picturesque city which is South Africa's only river port and the second largest coastal gateway to the province. Damian and Klara were interested in the historic past of Port Elizabeth, especially the landing place of the British settlers in 1820. They visited the Shamwari which is an award winning luxury game reserve, home for the "big five." Klara in particular visited the widely acclaimed, innovative and dynamic jewellers—Ritters proud of its roots in Port Elizabeth.

There was so much to see with so little time. However their quality time was spent discussing their intentions now that the tour was complete. They either return home or stay in South Africa for a while. There was fluidity in how long they could stay. Damian asked Klara "would you wish to stay on here for a little while longer?" She replied, "I am a bit concerned of people being knowledgeable of our winnings" but if Jason comes with a good proposition I would be happy for us to stay." Damian commented "we must speak with Jason and see how it would work because I do like Tsitsikamma very much."

Tsitsikamma Bay

They made a decision to call Jason. He showed great cordiality on the telephone. He said "I briefly discussed with my directors, but first they would like to meet both of you." "I could come with Mr Bradley Taylor one of my directors when it suits you," Jason asked "have you got your academic papers recommendations, passport, British Driving Licence and vaccination certificates with you?" Damian replied "we got all of these in our possession." They arranged a meeting date and time in a meeting room of the Tourist Bureau on the next day. Damian and Klara were elated and awaited the meeting.

Mr Brindley Taylor and Jason arrived in Port Elizabeth and met with Damian and Klara at the Tourist Bureau. They had pre-arranged the discussion room. Following formalities and introduction the four of them discussed the documents which were required by them. They spent almost two hours discussing work discipline, security and confidentiality towards the Water and Forestry Commission. Mr Taylor stated "if you are still interested to work I would appreciate both of you to spend two years to do a specific project, which would be allocated by the Commission." Mr Taylor was comfortable with Damian and Klara. He said "think about it and let me know" Jason assured them that free accommodation would be provided within the Forestry Commission acreage. Mr Taylor requested them to call Jason in the next couple of days.

Damian and Klara discussed the proposition with each other. Once they made the decision to stay in Tsitsikamma they called their respective parents and said that they would be taking up jobs offered by the commission. Yet again Damian's dad said "I am not so sure about your decision but if this is what you both want I give my blessings." Damian's mother came on the line and questioned "will you be able to return if you don't like it?" Damian said "we have an option to return home should we have concerns." On the other hand Klara's family were ecstatic. Her mum commented "We can arrange to visit you."

At the end of the week Damian called Jason and said "we have decided to take your offer" Jason said "That's good," Give me a couple of days and I can have the apartment ready" They arranged a date when Jason could collect them and return to Tsitsikamma. Damian arranged with Keith at the Bay Lodge hotel to extend their stay for a further couple of nights. Damian informed them that they would like to return to Tsitsikamma. He did not disclose that they would start work there.

Once arrangements were made Damian and Klara felt happy and had peace of mind. The next couple of days were spent relaxing, and reading about Tsitsikamma and its surroundings. Jason called in the following morning and requested them to be ready. He would arrive in two hours. After breakfast Damian and Klara got their luggage ready, checked out from the Bay Lodge Guest House and awaited Jason's arrival.

Jason arrived in his Land Rover and was happy to see them. After having helped Damian with the luggage, Jason assisted them to the vehicle and they set off for Tsitsikamma. Jason described the country en route and was happy to answer questions which they asked. On arrival at their destination they were shown their apartment. Damian and Klara were astonished that it consisted of a large veranda, two large bedrooms, a medium sized kitchen, a large bathroom/shower and toilet. Klara was very excited and said "all this for free." Jason explained that a houseboy will clean the apartment and a daily cook will help them with groceries, marketing and cooking. Damian said "this is too good to be true."

Jason said "since you are in possession of full British car licences we need to get you provisional licences to drive here. You need to however take it slowly as this country is not the safest place to drive." Mr Taylor provided them with work permits forms for completion.

Damian and Klara entered their apartment and had a rest in the afternoon. Jason invited them for the evening meal to his home where a delicious meal consisting of curry and rice was enjoyed by all. They had time for both social and purposeful conversation throughout the evening. They returned in Jason's vehicle at around 22.00hrs and made the way to their apartment. Damian spent sometime in each room so that he learned the location of electricity switches and gas switches. Although there was a telephone land-line both Damian and Klara called their families from their mobile phones prior to their sleep.

In the morning the cook who was called Rabi made them an omelette each with brown bread and tea. She originated in Somalia and was cheerful. The house boy was called Tom and he came from Cape Town. They both had a fair knowledge of English in order to communicate with Damian and Klara.

At around 09.00 hrs Jason came over to the apartment and drove Damian and Klara to the offices within the Water and Forestry Commission. Jason formerly introduced them to the National park. They were made comfortable in his large office. With the help of a large map of the forests Jason started his talk by saying "I hope you both will enjoy your work in one of the finest examples of preserved indigenous high forests in this country. The forests referred to here are those which we find in the coastal plateau between Tsitsikamma Mountains and the Indian Ocean from the keriboons River in the west and the Tsitsikamma river in the east. These forests are loosely termed the Tsitsikamma forests. These are in effect remnants of such larger forest expanses of the past. Today there remains only scattered patents of various sizes separated by agricultural lands and plantations of exotic trees." He continued explaining "the largest ten broken forest patches constitute the Lottering Forest of approximately 1800km. The history of the forests is basically one of over utilisation since 1711 and the sporadic attempts of conservation."

An Elephant at Addo national park

Damian and Klara began to learn that Jason was very knowledgeable and enthusiastic about his job. He was happy to answer their questions. He continued to explain in general about the six basic forest classifications the very dry scrub forest, dry high forest, medium moist high forest, moist high forest, wet high forest and the very wet high forest." Jason was keen to explain that the "general policy of the National Parks Board is one of total protection with limited utilisation for recreation. The primary objective is to maintain the forest ecosystem, while allowing a measure of utilisation of timber and other natural resources."

Jason continued "specific trees such the Red Alder, Tree Fuchsia, Cape Holly and the White Alder are protected flora. These require a permit from the Forestry and Water Commission for felling. Protected trees such as Stinkwood, Yellow Wood, White milk wood, White Banana and Forest Tree Fern are not felled or damaged without prior approval of the Commission."

As mentioned previously Jason was keen to let them know that the "conservation function of the Forestry Branch regarding the indigenous forests is based on multiple use management. Each forest compartment is allocated to the use of five management sections these are utilisation, protection, natural resources, recreation and research."

Jason stressed that "one cannot identify the different types of vegetation in a day, but in time you will be able to recognise these." He suggested that they have note books, make use of the many videos and photographs in the office library and most of all take the opportunity to talk with the competent staff and recognise specific species in reality."

A Lion at Shamwari Game Reserve

Chapter 4

As days and months passed by, Damian and Klara began to enjoy their work at the Forestry and Water Commission. Their official duties were from Monday to Friday 09.00 hrs to 17.00hrs. Saturdays and Sundays were free to spend at their leisure. They carefully selected areas to visit from the beginning.

The Eastern Cape Province has a matchless mix of culture, life styles, scenery, wildlife, vegetation, climate, floral richness and architecture. It is a land of staggering variety. The Eastern Cape Province is the birth place of President Mandela and is also the site of his Alma Mater-Fort Hare University which produced three Nobel Prize winners.

Meanwhile the families of both Damian and Klara were pleased that they had settled down. Mr Brindley Taylor informed them that each will be paid two hundred sterling pounds monthly and this will be back dated. Naturally Damian and Klara were very pleased. Mr Taylor was a straight talker but had much compassion.

Damian and Klara contributed much to their specific projects. Damian assisted a senior management team on ecosystem issues while Klara assisted the research team. In the domiciliary side Rabi and Tom worked well. They got on well together.

Almost five months had passed when Mr Brindley Taylor arranged to take Damian and Klara to the Augrabies National Park. It is believed that March to October were the best months to travel there. The Augrabies lie 120km west of Uppington and 30 km north-east of Kakamas, with national air links to Uppington. Access roads are tarred but the internal roads are not. Mr Taylor was happy to pay for their spacious air-conditioned accommodation.

The first sight of the 56m high Augrabies Falls fills one with awe. The spectacular sheer force of the largest South African River Orange as it cascades in a boiling, whirling, frothing torrent into a pool so deep is awesome. The sound of the thundering water swells as it picks its way over the lunar landscape of the barren road and the arid land.

The Park created to protect the Augrabies Falls and its surroundings was proclaimed in 1966 and has recently been extended to 82,000 hectares. The group joined a Game viewing safari. Springboks, Kudu, Klip-Springer were in plentiful. Damian and Klara appreciated Mr Taylor's gesture very much.

Damian and Klara made good their eight months at Tsitsikamma. It was the end of November and Klara's sisters made a trip to South Africa. Mr Taylor was happy to accommodate them in one of his guest houses close to his residence. Klara was ecstatic. When they arrived Damian and Klara spent their leisure time showing them the beauty spots in the Eastern Cape. They envied Klara and Damian. Soon they had to leave South Africa and return home before Christmas. Klara was somewhat moody since her sisters left but soon perked up to her normal self.

Damian and Klara spent Christmas with the Taylor family. He introduced them to many of his friends and colleagues. The company was stimulating and the food was sumptuous, not forgetting the delicious South African wine.

In late January of that year Klara felt unwell. Damian suggested that she should see a doctor. Dr (Mrs) Greta Agbo visited her at home. She was from Ghana and trained in England before she came to South Africa. On examination it was revealed that Klara could be two to three months pregnant. She saw Klara at her local clinic and advised her about nutrition, travel and safety. Dr Agbo promised to see her in four weeks time. Damian and Klara were very happy, but were concerned that they may have to leave South Africa. They discussed with Jason and Mr Taylor. They did not see it as a problem and affirmed that they continue to work. Klara informed her mother and sisters who requested her to return home, Damian however wanted her to remain in Tsitsikamma. The management was happy with them and their work. Jason promised to give Klara the best of care. After lengthy discussions with all concerned they decided to stay.

Although on earlier clinical examination Dr Agbo decided that Klara was two to three months pregnant. On her second examination a month later she found that her abdomen looked larger than expected for her dates. Dr Agbo accompanied Klara to the Port Elizabeth hospital maternity unit for a scan of her Uterus. While Klara lay on the bed the sonographer began the scan. Klara was tense and started to weep. Dr Agbo held Klara's hand and said "Klara look you have twins." Klara was in shock and tears rolled down her cheeks. She asked "are you sure?" Dr Agbo said "sure, sure." She then showed the scan. Later Klara told the sonographer "we have twins in my mother's family."

Dr Agbo and Klara returned to Tsitsikamma. Klara remained very quiet. She was thinking how Damian, her parents and sisters would take the news. Damian was anxiously waiting for them to arrive home. They welcomed each other and Dr Agbo. Damian said "well what's the news?" Klara blushed and said "I am definitely pregnant and the scan showed twins", Damian rushed forwards and hugged her. He said "I am so pleased." Dr Agbo said "Now Damian take good care of her" he said. "Certainly I will." Dr Agbo returned to the hospital having left, Damian and Klara to be with each other.

Around 21.00hrs Damian and Klara phoned their respective families. No doubt they were very happy for them but were concerned that they may not return to England. At around midnight they finally fell asleep. In the morning Damian met with Mr Taylor and Jason and he gave the good news. They congratulated both of them. Klara informed Mr Taylor that Dr Agbo would be talking to him concerning work and safety issues. Mr Taylor said "you could always do your research work in the office." He said "Enjoy being pregnant, remember it is not a disease." He began to laugh. Damian and Klara were happy with the arrangements. Klara was fit and enjoyed the food, practised her exercises and relaxed.

In March Mr Taylor invited Damian and Klara to join him, his wife and his nephew Nisa to visit the Kruger National Park, Klara got permission from Dr Agbo to fly and also travel by land. He pre-arranged accommodation in a self contained thatched cottage in the park. This was a treat for Damian and Klara.

Mr Taylor informed that the kruger national park was proclaimed a national park in 1926. It lies some 400km northeast of Johannesburg roughly the size of Wales or Massachusetts. The park occupies nearly 2000,000 hectares of the north-eastern Transvaal called Lowveld or Bushveld, to the north and south of the sanctuary two rivers, the Limpopo and the Crocodile respectively act as natural boundaries. To the east the Lebomo Mountains separate it from Mosambique. Its western boundary runs parallel with this range roughly 60km distant. The park varies in altitude between 200m in the east and 900m at Pretoriuskop in the south west. It is believed that six perennial rivers flow through this area.

A Cheetah at Kruger national park

The kruger national park offers more species of wildlife than any other African game sanctuary. There were camping and picnic spots with suitable facilities. Mr Taylor had pre-booked an organised tour for this group with a trained information officer, in a four wheeled drive vehicle. There was ample time for photography. The officer named as Sylvester explained that there were 137 species of mammals, 249 species of fish, 112 species of reptiles and 483 species of birds. The vegetation in the park consists of four main areas, the Thorn Trees, Red Bush Willow, knob

Thorn, Mopane and the Shrub Mopane. The film shows assisted in the camp site strengthened their knowledge further. The two days spent in Kruger were exhilarating.

While in the camp-site Damian walked to the toilet area when he saw a man walking quickly towards him. To Damian's surprise it was none other than Philip the driver who drove them through the Garden Route. He was taken aback. Philip said "hello, Mr Damian, how are you? Has Miss Klara come with you?" Damian said "yes" I am with a group and I need to get back," Just then Philip said "could you give me some money?" Damian replied "I haven't got much money" and handed a ten sterling pound note. At this Philip said "this is an insult when you have all that money from the winning." At this Damian said "look, I haven't got time to talk about money" and walked away. In the meantime Mr Taylor had seen Philip talking with Damian. He remarked "you must stop talking to strangers Damian." It is dangerous. This place is not England." Damian said "He was Philip who drove us to the Garden Route." Mr Taylor then replied "I suppose he asked for money." Damian said "as a matter of fact he did ask for money and I gave a ten sterling pound note." Mr Taylor said "now this will be a habit and he will somehow come after you" Mr Taylor said, "Its people like him who give South Africa a bad name" Klara was not happy She remarked "you should not have given any money Damian."

The group returned to Tsitsikamma unscathed. Klara looked tired. Damian and Klara appreciated Mr Taylor's generosity. During the coming weeks Dr Agbo monitored Klara's pregnancy. She examined her every two weeks. She suggested that "when Klara's pregnancy was thirty two weeks she has to be admitted to the maternity unit for a rest until the babies are born." She also informed them that "as far as she can assess it would be a normal birth but one never knows with twins. It could be a caesarean section." Klara was well prepared and appreciated the straight talk.

Klara and Damian's preparation began with shopping for baby clothes, maternity clothes, cradles and a twin pram to accommodate two babies. Both were excited as every day went by. She kept receiving parcels of her favourite food, and clothes, baby oil and cream from her family in England.

Dr Agbo was exceptionally able. She allocated a midwife to visit Klara every week. She was called Minnie who got on with both of them. In the meantime Klara's mother Maria was making preparations to be present for Klara's confinement. She was a Principal of a teacher training college and would be able to come over for two weeks.

Klara continued to take things quietly and spent more time at the office rather than go out to do field work, When time permitted she relaxed in the garden or veranda, Damian was very supportive of her and it was clearly visible that they loved each other dearly. One day when the house-boy Tom was in conversation with Klara he mentioned that Philip was his cousin and he had talked about them. This worried Klara no end. When Damian returned home she informed him about it. Damian said "One cannot get rid of Tom just because he is a relative of Philip." Damian was not overly concerned. Klara on the other hand saw it differently. "I am not at ease with this situation" "Damian reassured her you have nothing to worry about."

Dr Agbo continued to visit Klara. One morning she came with midwife Minnie. They both decided unanimously that Klara would have to enter the maternity unit at Port Elizabeth hospital in readiness for her confinement. On the next morning Dr Agbo, Minnie, Klara and Damian travelled to Port Elizabeth by car. Dr Agbo discussed the procedural matters with Damian and Klara, on the way to the hospital. Klara called her mum and requested her to come over to South Africa.

Klara spent three weeks in the maternity unit. She got to learn the new environment and the maternity staff. Named staff midwives were allocated to help in the confinement. Damian called her every day and visited her when he could. One afternoon when Klara woke up after a sleep, one of the nursing sisters known as Khadija said "you had a visitor but I did not let him in because you were asleep." "He called himself Philip and brought a bunch of flowers." Klara's face fell, "the sister asked "Are you alright?" Klara said "I have some back ache." Sister said, "I will ask one of the nurses to rub your back and also bring the flowers." Klara commented "thanks a lot." She was uncomfortable that Philip visited her but one cannot stop it. She informed Damian. All he had to say was "The Newswire is still working. Tom may be feeding information to Philip."

Impala at Kruger national park

Klara's mother Maria reached her destination. Klara was happy for her presence. During the next two days Klara got abdominal cramps. Dr Agbo was with her most of the time. Midwife Minnie was at her bedside too. One night Klara started with labour pains. Dr Agbo came immediately as she was on call. The Paediatricians and other Obstetricians were available should she have to go to the operating theatre for a caesarean section. In the early hours of the morning Klara gave birth to twin baby girls by normal delivery. They weighed six and a quarter and six and a half pounds each. The paediatrician Dr Roger Metcalfe declared that they were normal on examination. Damian and Maria were at her bedside all the way. Klara and Damian were delighted and thanked God for the normal outcome. Klara with tears rolling down her cheek thanked Dr Agbo and midwife Minnie. The obstetric team was keen for Klara to be in the maternity unit for longer. They felt that a new mum with two babies demand a lot from the mother.

Dr Agbo advised Damian to hire a children's nurse for a while. She suggested Sister Tracy an English nurse with paediatric qualifications. She was also a midwife. Klara spent ten days in the maternity unit and was supervised by the Scottish senior sister Marion. When it was time for Klara to leave the maternity unit, she and the babies were accompanied by Damian, Marion and Maria. Jason offered to drive them home.

The babies were identical twins and were named as Suzanna and Savannah. They always had their name tags on their wrists. Mr Taylor was at the apartment with a big basket of fruit. He welcomed them home. It was time for Klara's mother Maria to return in a couple of days owing to commitment to work. She did pay for all the professional services provided for Klara and her babies. Damian's face showed how proud he was to have Klara and the twins back home. He called his mum and Dad who were equally happy. Maria informed Klara's father and the sisters.

Sister Tracy supervised Klara and the babies for a month. This gave Klara real confidence to cope, with help from Damian. All the staff who assisted during the confinement received boxes of chocolates which Maria so kindly brought from England.

Chapter 5

As days passed by Suzanna and Savannah were thriving. They both had blonde hair and bright blue eyes. The only difference was that Savannah had a dark brown birth mark on her right forearm. Klara looked after the twins after sister Tracy left. Klara and Damian adored the little girls and took lots of photographs to send the family and friends. She arranged for Dr Roger Metcalfe to visit the twins fortnightly. He was happy with their progress. Damian registered their births at the Registry office in Port Elizabeth and included both in Klara's and Damian's passports.

In the meantime Klara and Damian discussed their future in South Africa. Although Mr Taylor and Jason were happy for them to stay on, Klara in particular wanted to return. When the twins were two months old they invited Mr Taylor to discuss their intentions. After giving them his ear Mr Taylor said "I am not going to stand in your way." Klara said "I would like to christen them in England." They informed both their parents that arrangements will be made for the family to return when the twins were five months old. The families were pleased and excited.

At the end of the two months they booked one way air tickets from Johannesburg to Manchester and gradually packed their personal belongings and collections. They already sent some of the packages as unaccompanied luggage.

The twins were putting on weight and getting responsive to the parents' voices and touch. Klara loved being mother to these beautiful twins. One afternoon around 16.00hrs Damian was at work, Klara fed the twins, made them comfortable and placed them in the pram on the veranda. She then asked Tom, the house boy to keep an eye on them. The twins were slowly going to sleep and Klara wanted a well earned shower prior to Damian returning home.

Seeni

A young Hyaena at Kruger national park

Klara showered herself and got dressed. She then came out of the room and called "Tom, where are you?" There was no answer. She then went to the kitchen and asked Rabi the cook "Could you please make me a cup of tea?" I don't know where Tom has gone." Rabi said "he may be in the toilet." All was quiet and she assumed that the twins were asleep and went onto the veranda and peeped in to the pram. To Klara's horror she saw one twin fast asleep but the other twin was not there." She called for Tom again and also Rabi. Tom finally came out of the toilet and Rabi came out of the kitchen. "Klara said "where is my baby?" Tom said "both of them were in the pram when I went to the toilet." She shouted at both of them. "Where is my child?" Klara was in hysterics and ran into the office crying and informed Damian what had happened. Damian came rushing out hastily and asked Tom and Rabi "what happened?" They both refused to answer any more questions. Klara was inconsolable. Jason came over and informed Damian that he had already called the local police and the British embassy in Cape Town. A team of police officers were already on their way. When the police arrived they took Tom and Rabi into custody. The police could not believe what had happened. They informed the Port Elizabeth Hospital, and a news item was broadcasted over South African

Television. Damian called Dr Agbo and Tracy. They came in a couple of hours. Damian and Klara also informed the police that it was Savannah who was abducted and that she had a dark brown birthmark on her right forearm.

Klara called her parents and gave the unexpected bad news. Klara's mum said "I will make arrangements for Zia to be with you as soon as I can." The British Consulate-General in Cape Town was very helpful. They had informed the Foreign office in London. Damian's father also spoke with the newspapers and the television News. Klara in the meantime was distraught. Dr Agbo prescribed medication so that she can get some sleep. Tracy took on the job of looking after Suzanna until Klara settled down.

Klara and Damian were so upset and started to argue. Klara believed that she was at fault for leaving the twins with Tom. Mr Taylor hired another cook call Esme and a house boy called Theodore to help Klara and Damian for the time being. Meanwhile Klara's sister Zia arrived within a week, and that made a big difference. Damian spent time with the police, the embassies, tourist bureau and children's homes. The police distributed leaflets far and wide. The police requested from Damian the Birth Certificates and Passports which Damian provided. The police kept visiting the apartment at different times of the day, to question Klara about the abduction. She was getting depressed having to repeat the same thing over and over again. Klara poured her heart out to Zia. She told her sister in a strange way "I knew 'something' would happen to take our joy away." Damian said very little to avoid any more minor conflicts between Klara and himself. They were extremely stressed.

In the meantime the English newspapers were full of Savannah's abduction and relatives kept sending letters of sympathy. Klara was visited by the British Consulate-General officials. They suggested that Klara and Suzanna should return home for their own safety while Damian could remain to assist the police. Klara, Damian and Zia discussed this proposition at length and the best way forward. Finally decision was made that Klara, Suzanna and Zia would leave Tsitsikamma within the week. Mr Taylor, Jason, the South African Police, the British Embassy did their best to make the departure a smooth one. A British Airways flight from Johannesburg was arranged and a stewardess was allocated to attend to

Klara and Suzanna on their journey. Damian looked so sad. He hardly made any conversation. At the airport he said "Klara, have a safe flight. I love you and will miss you dearly." Klara was sobbing all the way to the aeroplane. The last person she saw was Philip at the departure lounge. She pretended that she did not see him. The presence of Philip worried her in that he may harm Damian. All kinds of thoughts were going through her mind. She thought "How did Philip know that I was taking this flight?"

The long flight took its toll. Klara could not stop crying. Fortunately they were allocated business class seats which allowed some privacy. To add to all the sadness a very insensitive air stewardess brought a South African newspaper that had the story of Savannah on the front page. It also mentioned that they were lottery winners. Klara was literally sick. She was so glad that Zia was with her. Klara felt hopeless and helpless. Savannah was always on her mind. She kept saying "what if they kill her or hurt her?"

Klara, Suzanna and Zia were well looked after by the British Airways crew. It was a long flight. There to greet them were Klara's family, an official from the British Foreign office and two police officers. They spoke to Klara "We are here to help and protect you and your daughter. Please contact us anytime. Accommodation has been arranged for the three of you' in Manchester" We need to talk with you tomorrow when you would be less tired from the journey." Klara hugged her mother, father and sister Simoni. They had arranged another hotel for themselves. Hopefully they could see each other in the morning after the interview with the officials. Klara called Damian for a while from her mobile phone. She then fed Suzanna, settled her for the night and they all went to bed in the hotel.

Chapter 6

The following day was full of surprises. Damian called Klara and she wept. Klara received a bunch of red roses by Interflora from a well wisher. There was a mobile call from Philip the driver from Cape Town. Klara's sister answered the call and said "Klara is not here" Klara was scared. When the police officers met with her she informed about this call. The officer requested not to answer any calls from strangers. As Damian said the "newswire is still active."

In the afternoon Klara her sister Zia and baby Susanna travelled to Chipping, The rest of the family travelled in another vehicle. Klara and Suzanna settled in the family home. She called Damian on one day and he called her the next day. They discussed the developments but unfortunately Savannah was still missing. The South African police did intermittent television broadcasts to renew people's memories but in vain. Damian remained in South Africa for almost one month. Having discussed the issues with the British Ambassador and the South African police they requested him to return whenever the authorities needed him. They promised to keep him posted. Damian signed all the documents that they required and left the country.

On return Damian hired a Lawyer—Mr David Robinson. Damian and Klara had several meetings with him. Mr Robinson accompanied them to the British High commission, the Foreign Office and the South African Embassy and their Member of Parliament to put their case.

After a months lapse Damian, Klara and Suzanna were re-united as a family. This comforted them greatly. Klara was happy to have her family support but after six months in the family home, Damian suggested that it would be good to move to a home of their own. They looked for rented property and were able to have one which was near to Klara's parents' home. They hoped that in time they could buy a property and build their home to their specifications.

Damian started work at the University of Lancaster. His work experience in South Africa was an asset to his new post. Klara was happy to stay at home and care for Susanna. Leaving Susanna with others brought her bad memories.

Damian travelled to South Africa twice a year ever since they returned to England. Every day they hoped that there would be some news of Savannah. For the South African police Savannah was a statistic. For the British officials in South-Africa the trail had become cold. Damian and Klara prayed that she is alive and not hurt. This state of frustration played on their relationship.

As years went by, Suzanna grew older. When she was five years old and able to have some understanding, the parents explained to her that she had a sister who was just like her, but when they were both babies, one day she was missing from the pram. From that day onwards Suzanna used to talk to her sister when she played on her own, she included Savannah in her play, she kept drawing pictures of Savannah, she told her little friends in school about her and they thought she was odd. Klara and Damian explained to the Head Teacher, about the circumstances when she started school, hoping they would understand her. Some of her teachers however had soon forgotten that information.

As Suzanna got older she kept questioning her parents about Savannah. This hurt them both. One day when Suzanna was fifteen years old, she said "mum, it is your fault that Savannah is missing" "Now I have no sister because of you." Klara was very upset at this remark. She spoke with her General practitioner who had much empathy. He referred her to Dr (Mrs) Solomon, a psychologist who said to have an interest in this area. Accompanied by Dr Solomon Klara went along to the missing children's bureau, and placed her photograph of Savannah and also arranged counselling for her.

Life continued with the constant knowledge of a hole in their hearts. Damian and Klara bought a converted barn in Chipping close to Preston and had a comfortable living. They made good friends who stood by them.

Life was very difficult for the whole family. They had money but not much happiness. When Suzanna was eighteen years old, she entered the University of Lancaster to do a degree in Travel and Tourism. One day she told her parents "may be I could visit South Africa and find out about 'missing' Savannah." Day by day Suzanna distanced herself from her mother. She could not forgive her mother who in her eyes left them unattended. On several occasions Damian had to explain to Suzanna that it was not her mother's fault. Suzanna then said "so you are both in this together" Klara was heart broken.

Suzanna was a bright student and obtained a first class Honours Degree. She looked well at the Degree Ceremony and Klara and Damian were so proud of her. Before she went to the ceremony she made a remark "it would have been so good if we both graduated together." Savannah always played on her mind what ever she did. Following her graduation Suzanna did not start a job. She said to her parents "I would like to see the place where I was born and also see the place where Savannah went missing." Damian agreed and arranged for the three of them to travel to Cape Town and then to Tsitsikamma. Damian spoke with the British Consulate-General in Cape Town and the Police. Since twenty years had passed the officers had moved on. However he managed to meet with the present officers during their stay. Mr Taylor, Jason and Dr Agbo had retired. Klara and Damian had no direct contact with any one they knew before. Officials from both organisations promised to renew their search for Savannah. Klara brought Suzanna's photographs hoping someone might have seen Savannah in her adult life as they were twins. They were informed by the police that even Interpol was involved in the search for Savannah.

Having spent a week in Cape Town the family made a trip to Tsitsikamma in a hired car. They met the director Mr Benjamin Greaves and the manager Mr Kiru of the Forestry and Water Commission by appointment. They were aware of the circumstances. However they were new appointments. They read the incident notes from their previous records but were unable to give them new information. Klara informed them yet again "Susanna my daughter who you see now and Savannah who went missing are identical twins and she would be like Suzanna now."

Damian asked Mr Greaves' permission to have a look around the apartment they had lived. There was no objection to the request. The family looked around the garden and apartment which had not changed much. Suzanna was very pensive. Damian commented "this is the veranda from which Savannah went missing" Suzanna then said "Oh God please bring her back." Klara was saddened. She sobbed all the way. She said, "I hope she is alive somewhere."

Just as they were about to leave the Tsitsikamma compound, a man bumped into Klara. She said to Damian "His face is familiar" This man was around forty years of age. He was dark in complexion and had a beard. It was difficult to recognise him. Damian saw him quickly moving on and said to Klara "that was Tom the house-boy." Klara then said "yes, it is him." Suzanna remarked "it is strange how he ran away so quickly." The family then returned to the office of Mr Greaves the director and asked him "does Tom still work for you?" He said "yes, do you know him?" Klara commented "it was Tom who kept an eye on the twins while I had a shower." Mr Greaves said "Tom has health problems and has been in hospital many times. He has mental illness but spends two days a week here doing odd jobs for us." Klara, Damian and Suzanna looked at each other. Mr Greaves said "Tom is unreliable but I will talk to him." Damian was quite puzzled by Tom's behaviour. The family returned to Cape Town and informed the official at the Embassy of how they had a close encounter with Tom. They said that this information was important and it will be checked out.

They returned home to England with not much information about Savannah, but felt that it may be a pointer in the right direction if only Tom could talk. Suzanna said "now I know where I was born and where Savannah went missing. Dad, we need to get to the bottom of this." To think that I have sister is amazing, but not knowing where she is hurts me." Klara said "in my heart there was a certain feeling that Tom knew what happened to Savannah but it was only a feeling" On their return to England the family believed that the search for Savannah had got cold. Damian discussed with his lawyer Mr Robinson who would contact the Foreign Office. They had to re-open the case once again. All this was frustrating to the family.

Klara tried so very hard to brave the situation. She somehow was unable to speak of her feelings to Damian. In his own way Damian tried not to have any arguments with Klara. Suzanna understood the situation and played fair by all. Klara spent much of her time writing poetry. In that way she was able to express her feelings. She thought one day she may be able to publish them. Although many years have passed by, the family 'lives' the abduction of Savannah as if it was yesterday. Their heartache is too much to bear. Their only hope is that every phone call or every letter may bring Savannah close to them. Klara in particular lives with a feeling of guilt that she left her babies without adult supervision. Now her trust in people has gone forever.

Chapter 7

Life without Savannah left a huge hole within the family. Damian continued his work at the University. He was now the Principal lecturer in his department. Suzanna was an air stewardess for Virgin airways. This situation left Klara at home. She was unable to hold a job owing to her bouts of depression and anxiety. She continued to go for counselling sessions. She continued writing poetry and this allowed her to express herself. Friends who read her work were very complimentary.

About five months following their trip to South Africa something unprecedented happened. At around 18.00 hours one evening Klara answered the land line telephone. At the other end of the phone was a foreign voice saying "is that Miss Klara?" She replied "yes." who are you?" He said "my name is Philip" Klara nearly put the phone down but hesitatingly kept hanging on to it. He continued "I am the driver who drove you to "the Garden Route" many years ago." Klara said "ah, yes I remember." Philip replied "I got your telephone number from Mr Greaves at the Forestry and Water Commission. I want to speak with Mr Damian to give him some news." Please take down this telephone number and ask him to give me a call" he then discontinued the call.

Klara was alone at home and got anxious. She called her mother who came to her in about fifteen minutes. They waited for Damian to arrive home. On his arrival Klara conveyed the message to him. They had their evening meal and Damian said "wonder what it is?" I am not so sure that I want to have discussions with him" Klara's mother said "I think you should call him and hear his story." Klara kept silent. Damian said "may be I should. Let me relax for ten minutes I had a challenging day."

Damian called on the number Philip had given to Klara. No one answered it. In half an hour he called again and a man answered the phone. Damian said "could I please speak with Philip?" The voice said "ah Mr Damian, the reason I want to speak with you is this. My nephew Tom said to me that he thought he recognised Miss Klara, you and another girl in Tsitsikamma some months ago. He is suffering from mental illness and he may have forgotten, but yesterday as he talked to me and mentioned that some relatives he is friendly with had seen a white girl with a family. These people I know are in Sudan." "The Only problem is that I need you to give me some money so that I can get round Tom. He can then give detail information about these people." As Klara heard Philip speak she began to weep. Klara's mother supported her. Damian replied "I will think about this and be in touch." Suzanna was on a flight to New York. When she reached her destination Klara called on her mobile phone and gave her the news. She was shocked. Klara said "please don't divulge this to anyone."

In the morning Damian called the Foreign office to convey the gist of the telephone call from Philip. Damian and Klara discussed what they should do now. In the morning Damian called Philip again. He asked "do you know these friends of Tom." Philip said "no, but Tom will direct me to these people. I can then take you to them" First you must give me £25,000 and not tell the police as this is a delicate situation."

The next day was spent planning strategies for progress. Damian spoke with his family and Mr Robinson his lawyer. He suggested that he could accompany Damian to South Africa but the Foreign office must be aware of it. He called the Foreign Office and they said that their colleagues in Cape Town would be informed about their trip.

Damian's father volunteered to make the trip. Klara was not well to make such a trip. Arrangements were made for them to leave for Cape Town. Their visa applications were helped by the Foreign Office and they booked three return open tickets to Cape Town. Damian met with the Bank manager and discussed his journey. Mr Robinson suggested that Damian should take with him, photographs of the twins as babies and a photo of Suzanna as an adult. He also took with him their Birth Certificates. He requested Damian to refrain from getting into deep conversation with passengers on the flight.

Damian was glad of his father's and Mr Robinson's support. It took them more than a week to sort out all the arrangements. Finally they took a British Airways direct flight to Cape Town. It was a long flight and Damian, his father and Mr Robinson discussed their plans. As requested their first port of call was the British Consulate-General. The on-call official was waiting for them. He had already pre-booked two hotel rooms on their behalf. He suggested that they need to meet with Philip in day light hours.

Damian, his father and Mr Robinson checked in at the Belle Vue hotel and relaxed after dinner. In the morning after Breakfast Damian called Philip and requested him to meet the group at the Waterfront visitor centre. At around 10.30 hrs Philip turned up and shook their hands Damian introduced his party by name only. They sat down in a room of the Visitor Centre and immediately discussed business at hand. Philip started by saying "My nephew Tom said that he would introduce you to his friends who know where your daughter is." "If you are happy for me to do my part of the deal now, I can take you to Tom. He is here in Cape Town." Damian said "I believe he is mentally ill. "How do I know if Tom is truthful?" "Mr Damian he is not insane, he will talk to you and say what he knows" Damian reluctantly said "Philip, I will give you half of what you wanted. Once Savannah is found I will give the rest." Philip thought for while and said "alright then Mr Damian, I will take £12,500." Damian gave a packet to Philip; Damian said "please count that it is correct." Philip did so. He then said "please get into the car we will collect Tom and go. It is only a few miles away."

Two plain clothed British Consulate-General officials were not too far from them. However, Tom was unaware of them. The first stop was Tom's home. Philip introduced the group. Tom was silent throughout. Philip asked him to get into the people carrier. They resumed their journey towards a shanty town. Philip, Tom and Damian got out of the vehicle and entered a small house. Mr Robinson stayed in the vehicle. A weak old man and his pretty wife requested them in. There was not much space but they squeezed themselves in. The man was called Jerome and the wife was called Letitia. Jerome said "Twice a year my wife and I travel to Juba in the Sudan to see our relatives. The last time we were there we saw a pretty young white skinned girl with another man and woman. The young woman had white hair meaning (blonde). She was quite tall and thin. We were all in the market so I saw at close distance. We also saw the house they went into after shopping" she had a dark brown birthmark on her right forearm." At this Damian knew it was Savannah. Jerome and his wife were gentle people and Damian trusted them. I can take you there but it is a long way. We have to get visas. Damian said "thank you very much, I will make arrangements and let you know."

The group got back into the vehicle and returned to Cape Town. While they were in the car Philip said to Damian. "So you did not believe me when I told you about this." Damian replied "yes it is hard to believe anyone these days" Thank you Philip I will contact you when arrangements are made to travel to Sudan." Philip said "Jerome and I will accompany you if you can get the tickets for us. Sudan is a dangerous place to go." Damian, his father and Mr Robinson alighted from the vehicle in the city and strolled along the streets until they entered a restaurant to have some dinner.

Damian called the on-call Embassy official. He advised Damian to meet with him at 10.00hrs on the next day. At dinner they discussed about Sudan. Damian said "I really don't know much about the place. Damian's father was quietly optimistic. They made calls to their loved ones but did not raise hopes. All they said was "there is some progress." Mr Robinson explained that he would have to return to England owing to pressing engagements. However he advised Damian as much as he could before he departed in the morning.

Damian said to his father "All these years I distrusted Philip and now in a strange way I have begun to believe what he says." On the following morning Damian and his father walked into the British Embassy. There they met with the official and related the meeting with Jerome and his wife.

The two officers who followed them into the shanty town had expert knowledge of kidnap and ransom. They were concerned that Damian parted with a large sum of money. However they had a gut feeling that this thread was genuine and should be followed. They informed Damian that the UNCHR office in Juba may help them.

Damian and his father's stay in Cape Town had to be extended. The British embassy took care of the visa issue. They informed that one of the officers would accompany Damian. It took over one week for all the documentation and air tickets to be arranged.

During the week that was spent in Cape Town, Damian and his father spent much time researching about Sudan. None of them knew much except that it was in Africa. However they learned that Sudan is a country in north eastern Africa, bordered by Egypt to the north, the red sea to the northeast, Eritrea and Ethiopia to the east, Kenya and Uganda to the south east, republic of the Congo and the Central African Republic to the southwest, Chad to the west and Libya to the northwest. The world's longest river—the Nile divides the country between east and the west. The Blue and the White Nile rivers meet at Khartoum to form the river Nile which flows northwards through Egypt to the Mediterranean Sea. The capital Khartoum serves as the political, cultural and commercial centre of the nation. Omdurman is the largest city.

A member of the United Nations Sudan also maintains membership with the African Union, the Arab league as well as serving as an observer in the world trade organisation. Its legal system is based on English common law and Sheria law. Recent history informed Damian about the Darfur war and the civil war in Chad.

Reading what follows upset Damian. The US govt (21. Oct 2002) Sudan Peace Act accused Sudan of genocide in the second Sudanese civil war,(1983-2005) which has cost more than 2 million lives and displaced more than 4 million people. It is estimated that more than 200,000 people have been taken into slavery during the war.

They learned that Juba is the capital of southern Sudan and is a river port which became an independent country on the 9th July 2011. As of April 2009 Juba's airport is the site of large numbers of flights bringing United Nations and staff from non-governmental organisations (NGO) as well as general air freight.

Damian and his father felt uneasy having read the information above, but they were now aware of the terrain and felt stronger to face what came their way. In and around the centre of Juba they saw foreign nationals, some smiled at them but others stared. At the back of their mind was the advice from the Officials to keep their counsel. What they did enjoy was the delicious spicy food in the restaurants.

Chapter 8

The British Consulate-General official made arrangements for return air tickets to Juba for Philip, Jerome, Damian and his father. The official, Damian and his father would have hotel accommodation. Jerome and Philip will be accommodated in the home of Jerome's relatives. They took a South African Airways flight to Khartoum and then to Juba. They checked in, got settled in the Sunset hotel. In the evening the official contacted Philip and requested Jerome to show the house where the girl has been seen. They met at the hotel and hired a taxi. Jerome quickly commented "I will show the house and then I will go to my relatives."

The officer and Damian had a plan which they would follow. Jerome would accompany them and show the house. The officer commented "that's all we need from him." Damian, his father and Philip would remain in the car. The officer would knock on the door and speak to who ever was there. These instructions were noted by all.

At around 17.00 hours the officer knocked on the door. An English speaking gentleman opened the door and greeted him. He was around fifty years old had a South African accent and a tanned complexion. The officer introduced himself as David Fenton. The gentleman introduced himself as Theo Baldwin. "My wife and daughter are out." Mr Baldwin said "I work for the UNCHR in Juba and my daughter also works with the NGOs."

Mr Baldwin said "Please take a seat" He commented, "What may I ask is your reason for this visit?" This was a very sensitive issue. Mr Fenton took great care in replying. "I have come here to discuss a very delicate problem. I work for the British Consulate-General in Cape Town and we have been informed that twenty years ago identical twin girls were born to a couple known as Damian Sinclair and Klara Klaber in the maternity hospital Port Elizabeth. At that time this couple were contracted to the Tsitsikamma

Forestry and Water Commission." "The facts as we understand are that one twin went missing while a sleep in a double pram from the veranda of their apartment." Mr Baldwin listened attentively to Mr Fenton, "For the past twenty years the parents have searched for the little girl who was only two months old at that time. It is now suggested that she is with you as your child. By law the Consulate-General has to make enquiries. That is the reason I am here." The Embassy in Khartoum is aware of my visit today.

Mr Baldwin immediately started talking. His voice was faint. "Martha, my wife and I have tried for a child for many years but failed. We were looking for a child for adoption when we were informed that a white child was brought to the orphanage in Juba. He continued "we were given to understand that the baby was brought by a man who found her on the roadside following a horrific car accident. All the occupants in the crash had died." He continued "we paid a large sum of money to the orphanage at that time and took her and loved her dearly as our own" Beyond that I have no other information." Mr Fenton then asked him "Have you got a photograph as she is now?" Mr Baldwin walked to the dining room and produced a large framed photograph and another unframed photograph." Mr Fenton asked "has she got any specific birth marks on her body?" Mr Baldwin said "yes, she has a dark brown birth mark on her right forearm." The framed photograph demonstrated a tall slightly tanned young woman with blonde hair and blue eyes like Suzanna. Mr Fenton asked Mr Baldwin "What name have you given to her?" He replied 'Anastasia'. He then asked Mr Baldwin "have you disclosed to the girl the truth of her existence in your home?" He replied. "Yes the truth as I know."

Mr Fenton asked "may I take this photograph for our records?" Mr Baldwin said "so long as you return it." Mr Fenton asked "where about is the orphanage?" Mr Baldwin commented, "The orphanage caught fire three years ago. The general feeling is it was arson. Many children died along with the director. It was three miles from here" Gathering information took just over an hour. It was very tense. Mr Fenton said "thank you for the information, It has been most useful, should we need further information I will contact you, perhaps I could have your business card." Mr Baldwin obliged. They said their goodbyes. Mr Fenton made an exit from the house and had to walk a few hundred yards to where the vehicle was parked. He got into the car and said "That was useful and nothing more."

They retuned to the hotel in Juba. Mr Fenton spent time with Damian and his father. He said "these are early days I have to get the ball rolling." Mr Fenton showed the photograph of his daughter Savannah to Damian. He gazed at it and took the photograph of Suzanna from his case and said "They are identical." Mr Fenton agreed. Although Mr Fenton agreed that the twin was Savannah it was somewhat difficult for him to believe Mr Baldwin's story. "The embassy will follow a strategy and communicate with you and the police. I would please advise you to hold your counsel until these sensitive matters are ironed out, If and when I require you and your family to return I shall communicate this with you."

Mr Fenton, Philip, Damian and his father took the return flight late in the evening to Cape Town. Damian gave the rest of the deal to Philip. "Mr Damian, if you ever need me please do not hesitate to contact me." Damian and his father returned to their hotel and had dinner in a restaurant by the marina. While having dinner they discussed this whole episode. They were so grateful that Savannah is alive. Both called their families, but as advised by Mr Fenton was very careful in what they said. Damian said "I will see you soon." The early morning flight from Cape Town reached Manchester International airport in the early hours of the evening on the next day. Klara and Suzanna were there to meet them.

So much has happened in the past few days that Damian spent time with the family narrating the story so far. The extended family made frequent visits to inquire details about the visit to South Africa and Sudan. The advice of Mr Fenton however, was at the back of their minds at all times. They were relieved but it was not all over yet. These were anxious days.

Chapter 9

Days and months passed since their return from South Africa. At times the family was ecstatic that Savannah was alive at times they felt helpless and hopeless. Communications from the British Embassy was far and few between. When Damian contacted the Foreign office all they had to say "be patient there is much work to be done." At times hope was gone but they believed that Savannah was alive and well. They wanted to pour their thoughts and emotions to their friends but they were instructed not to do so. They were always aware that the officials had to progress this situation with much diplomacy.

Suzanna continued with being an air stewardess and Damian was busy at the University. However Klara was depressed and she was losing weight. It was difficult for her to cope but she carried out her daily chores. As the autumn leaves were falling, the cool evenings and the chill of the winds did not help the family. One evening Klara answered a telephone call. It was Mr Fenton. He said "please could the three of you arrange to travel to Cape Town in the next fortnight." You must contact my office on arrival. You need to be here for a week or more." Klara said "yes, most certainly." She hesitated to ask any questions. Klara called Damian immediately. Suzanna was on a flight to Dubai. When Damian returned home they discussed the arrangements. He had to take leave from the University. Damian left a message for Suzanna to call home as soon as possible. They also discussed the arrangement with their respective families and once again reminded them to keep their counsel.

When Suzanna arrived home, Damian and Klara were able to make a definitive arrangement. They booked the return flight with British Airways, pre-booked the Belle Vue hotel at the Waterfront Cape Town and took the early morning flight. On arrival at Cape Town Damian contacted the British Embassy.

Mr Fenton along with another official named Mr Barrington-Hines met with the family in a private room in the Consulate-General's office. Mr Fenton began with saying "we are sorry this has taken so long. There was much diplomacy involved. The reason is that Mr and Mrs Baldwin had not disclosed to Savannah that they were not their biological parents. This prevented us from proceeding further until the Police intervened. The result was Mr and Mrs Baldwin admitted to Savannah that she was adopted. Savannah was named Anastasia by them. The police had also found that the story about the orphanage was untrue. The police had to interview, Philip, Tom and Jerome many times until they came out with the truth." Mr Fenton explained "Tom is severely ill and his responses to questions have been unreliable. Philip had disclosed that he was only trying to help Damian and Klara and had not taken part in kidnapping the child. Jerome had no ulterior motive in saying what he observed."

Mr Barrington-Hines then took over the discussion from Mr Fenton. He said "Mr and Mrs Baldwin will be glad to meet with you all. We will act as mediators during the meeting" He explained "Savannah (Anastasia) has a birth certificate but we have checked with the maternity hospital at Port Elizabeth hospital and the date of birth is incorrect. Details of the birth certificate you provided are correct. We and the police have no hesitation in declaring that Savannah is your child. The only evidence we are unable to demonstrate is how and who kidnapped the baby. It is up to both families to agree the progress from now on. Most of all Savannah is of age where she can make up her own mind. Damian thanked both the officials." Mr Fenton commented "I will make arrangements for you all to travel to Juba and call you."

Two days later a call from Mr Fenton informed them that a South African flight to Juba has been arranged. The family was excited but apprehensive. While on their way to Juba Suzanna told Klara, "Mum, please don't start crying when we meet them, we need to be strong" Damian said "I wonder if the Baldwin family prepared Savannah for this meeting." On arrival at Juba they checked in at the same hotel they were in the last time they were here. Mr Fenton and Mr Barrington-Hines met them at the hotel and picked them up to visit Mr and Mrs Baldwin.

At around 18.00 hrs Mr Fenton knocked on the front door of the home of the Baldwin family. They had already been notified of the visit. Mr Baldwin opened the front door. He said "please come in, this is my wife Martha and daughter Anastasia." After the introductions were complete, Savannah (Anastasia) said "I have now seen my twin sister." She moved towards her and hugged her. Suzanna gave her the large box of chocolates she brought from England. After some "small talk" Mr Fenton said to Savannah "May be you could meet the family in the hotel and have a chat." Damian commented "that would be good." Klara remained quiet throughout the meeting.

On the next morning Savannah made a call to the hotel. Damian answered. She said "Is it alright for me to drop by in an hour?" He said "most certainly, our flight to Cape Town is at 16.00 hrs." When she arrived they greeted each other and had a cup of coffee. Savannah said "All this is too much for me. I need to make a decision as to what I ought to do now. I would like to visit England and get to know my real parents. I am very happy here and don't want to upset anyone" Damian said, "Take your time we are always there for you whenever you wish to see us." They spent about two hours in the hotel. Savannah gave her mobile number and the land number to Damian. Suzanna also gave her telephone numbers. Klara held Savannah and gave her a kiss. Savannah then left the hotel.

At around 15.00 hrs Mr Fenton and Mr Barrington-Hines met them at the airport. Damian said "we met Savannah in the morning and the meeting went smoothly." He said "we are satisfied that the developments went as expected so far. Mr Fenton said we will take care of Savannah and her interests should she wish to visit England. "My office will be in touch with you."

Damian, Klara and Suzanna boarded their return flight from Juba to Cape Town and then to Manchester as arranged. They were almost in shock for having seen and talked with Savannah. Klara said "they are identical but Savannah is tanned." Damian remarked "She seems a strong girl who knows what to do" Suzanna remarked, "It is so strange to see another person exactly like me." Damian said "for the time being we may not have sleepless nights."

Following their return home to England they were somewhat relaxed. The family was able to talk to friends and family about their long lost daughter. Emotions that they held on for so long were let out sometimes with tears and at times with smiles and laughter. As weeks and months went by letters were exchanged between the family and Savannah. Telephone calls were initiated by both sides. It made the family feeling somewhat light hearted.

Three months went by and Savannah decided to visit England for eight weeks. She said "I am anxious to chat with you all and meet my relatives. I want to relate my experiences and discuss your life without me." There was no mention if she would come here for good. Damian was keen that none of them pushed Savannah too far. He said "she has grown up making her own decisions, she is well educated and we must respect it, we need to give her enough space and allow her to make her own decisions."

Klara was keen that she had the best bedroom in the house. She began to organise the décor prior to her arrival. When Savannah was ready to visit England, Mr Fenton called Damian and said "We feel that it would be safe if you could accompany Savannah to England from Cape Town. Also it would help both of you." After talking to Klara, Damian spoke with Savannah and said "I will accompany you from Cape Town." They discussed the flight numbers and all other arrangements were finalised Klara was ecstatic. Suzanna said "I need to get some time off from work."

Following a call from Mr Fenton, Damian set off on his journey to Cape Town, where he will meet Savannah at the Belle Vue hotel. Damian could not believe that Savannah is alive and he will see her. He reached Cape Town and took a taxi to the hotel where he met Savannah and Mr Fenton. He said "I am so glad that you can accompany your daughter. There will be much time to get to know each other" Damian and Savannah simultaneously said "certainly." Mr Fenton left the hotel. Damian and Savannah settled down to sleep after dinner. In the morning they got ready for the flight.

On the British Airways flight to Manchester they had time to talk. It appeared that Savannah was an avid reader and completed a master's degree in architecture and town planning. She worked at the UNCHR office (United Nations High Commission for Refugees) as an NGO. She was interested to know about Damian's work at the University. Damian explained about Suzanna's interest in tourism and travel. He gently explained "Klara has not been too well ever since you went missing and still after twenty years she thinks it was her fault." Savannah said "yes, I do understand dad and will bear that in mind." Damian and Savannah got on well during the flight.

Savannah was excited that she was actually landing in Manchester. Although she had travelled to the African countries she had not been to Europe. At around 20.00 hours Damian and Savannah landed in Manchester International airport and there to meet them were Klara and Suzanna. There were hugs and kisses all round. Suzanna helped with the luggage and she drove them to Chipping in Lancashire where a delicious meal awaited father and daughter.

Chapter 10

After a restful night Savannah said "I cannot believe that I am England." I was so anxious before I arrived." The family sat in the drawing room later and discussed what Savannah would like to do. She said "let us, talk and talk and talk." They did talk most of the time but Damian set out a programme where she could be inducted to Lancashire. They had many rides to the countryside which Savannah enjoyed. Susanna accompanied her to the shops, cinema, libraries, her friends and relatives.

The family spent time in many country restaurants and talked about their experiences without Savannah. She said "and I did not know anything about your sadness." Damian said "it was not your fault I suppose we were unlucky not to have you for so long. You are alive and well and that's what matters." She said "Mr and Mrs Baldwin loved me and gave me a good education. They taught good manners, values and to be independent. They were always supportive." When Damian and Klara had some quality time together they wondered how their lives would change, if she were to settle down here. It was a sensitive subject and too soon to discuss this with Savannah.

Savannah was an avid reader and loved books. Damian accompanied her to the book shops and she bought some books of wild life, and the British Isles. During the eight weeks in England the family accompanied her to many parts of the U.K. She was excited about Edinburgh in particular. In London she was able to see the old and new buildings and appreciated both types in the city. She was glad to see a few shows in the West End of London.

It was inevitable that the family and Savannah were sussing out each other. One day Suzanna went to her mum and whispered "Savannah is not a bit like me, she knows so much about other countries and life in general, she is very grown up." Klara said "yes its only natural our world expands with travel, but you will know many things that she has not encountered in her life, so the more you exchange ideas with her the more you would get closer." Savannah was excited when she talked about Africa. She discussed African geography, politics, ethnicity and culture.

As weeks passed by Savannah appeared to grasp the life in Lancashire. Damian commented how knowledgeable she was in world affairs. In the main she had empathy with the poor, fallen and down trodden people. She had worked as an NGO with the planning division of the UNCHR and this experience had widened her scope in and around the world. Klara and Suzanna were keen to buy her clothes and jewellery but Savannah declined. One day Savannah said "I am not interested in fashion and style. I am not material minded. When I see so many people who have nothing to eat or drink and no where to live, buying goods for me sickens me." I suppose living in Africa all my life has made me realise about my values which are so different from those in the western world." It is so good of you to give me the opportunities should I want them."

Savannah had plenty to talk with the family. She also visited her close relatives which made her happy. In the meantime Suzanna resumed her work in the airlines and was on long flights. Before Suzanna left for her flight Savannah plucked up courage and said "I know you love me a lot, you spent your whole life looking for me. Finally you found me and you may wish me to live here in England." Damian immediately commented "Yes, that was our intention but having met you we realise that life here is so very different from what you have experienced. Even if you want to continue living in South Africa, we are happy that you are alive and well." Savannah replied "This is very difficult for me. I tried to think like a European but I am not able to. My values are different from you. I am devoted to the African people. They have very little money, food and shelter but they are able to share what they got with those who are less fortunate. They carry their love for others in their hearts. People take me for what I am, not for the clothes I wear. Although I know you love me dearly, my heart says I will have to go." Suzanna was speechless. Klara had tears in her eyes. It took Damian to say "Thank you Savannah we do appreciate you for airing what your heart felt. We appreciate it. We have lost you once and don't want to lose you again. We will always be there for you." Savannah commented "I am so grateful to my other parents, what you see in me is due to them. I am only very sad that Mr and Mrs Baldwin did not tell me the truth. I will always be in touch with you by phone or letter. "I promise that I will come again."

Damian and Klara discussed about gifting her some money before she left. Damian said "I would like to give you some money of what is left of our lottery winning" Savannah replied "No dad I don't need money. I get well paid, and I have a comfortable life in terms of African standards." Later Damian said to Klara "It was somewhat disappointing but again we must try to understood her values."

While Savannah was in England Philip made a social telephone call to Damian. He said "I am glad you found your daughter. I thought I will let you know that while Savannah was with you there has been a story about her and the family she lived with in Juba." It has been in most of the Sudanese and South African news papers." I thought I would let you be aware of this." Damian had to let Savannah know the gist of the conversation. She was very upset.

Within the next week Damian arranged a single flight to Juba for Savannah and a return flight to Manchester for himself. Klara felt that Damian's support during the flight would indeed help her. Damian called the British Embassy in Cape Town and informed Mr Fenton of their arrival. He was somewhat taken aback that Savannah was returning so quickly. Damian indicated that she needs time to get her thoughts together.

The day before Savannah and Damian left for South Africa, the family went out to a cosy restaurant for dinner. Suzanna returned from her flights and was able to make it too. Savannah thanked them all for making her stay comfortable and most of all for continuing to look for her all these years. She hugged Suzanna and said "We must meet up in Africa. I will show you the best parts in Sudan and also the Nile. I feel so calm when I see the Nile." Suzanna held back her tears and said "yes that's a promise." Damian held them both and gave a hug. Klara continued to take photographs at every opportunity during Savannah's stay here.

On the day of departure Suzanna drove the family to Manchester airport. There was not much conversation during the hour long journey. At the airport Suzanna and Klara hugged and kissed both Savannah and Damian. They wished them a safe journey. Klara continued to weep. Suzanna said "mum, thank God that we have found her. We will be able to see her again soon."

The flight allowed both Damian and Savannah to learn more about each other. Damian brought with him Savannah's birth certificate and a copy of the page on his passport which included her as a child. He gave it to her for safe keeping. Savannah commented "Now I have two Christian names and surnames, two passports and two birth certificates. Damian said "be in touch with the British Consulate-General's office. They will support you."

During the flight Damian asked Savannah "Do you have many friends?" she said "most of my colleagues at work are my friends. We all support one another because most of them come from different countries. I am interested in wildlife and we go on safari together. She continued "the terrain is generally flat plains broken by several mountain ranges in the west. Jebel Marra is the highest range. In the south is mount Kinyeti Imatong near the border with Uganda. In the east are the Red Sea hills. She said "I love the Blue Nile, it is so majestic." Damian observed that her love of Africa came from within.

The long flight to Cape Town was made short by the conversation and laughter with father and daughter. To Damian, Savannah was a breath of fresh air. She was full of life and Damian enjoyed the encounter which he missed for twenty years.

When they reached the airport arrivals section, they were shocked at the presence of photographers taking pictures of them. Savannah in particular said "dad these people will put this in the papers." My, how news go round" Damian said. "If any journalist approach you please don't talk." The "newswire" was after me and Klara now they are focusing on you" Having reached Cape Town in the evening Damian and Savannah checked in at the Belle Vue hotel. In the morning they both met with Mr Fenton at the British Embassy. Savannah took her flight at.11.00 hours to

Juba. It was heart breaking for Damian. Savannah hugged him and said "I won't say goodbye but say "au revoir." "I will be in touch. Thank you, mum and Suzanna for finding me. Love you." Damian said "Take good care of yourself, we all love you dearly."

As Savannah checked-in for her flight, Damian saw this tall willowy figure of his daughter slowly fading away in the distance. She looked back twice and may have seen her dad still there. Damian wished that she could have remained in England. He had to wait in the departure lounge for another hour to check-in for his flight to Manchester. He made a short mobile call to Klara. He then went to the newsagent to buy a newspaper and to his horror the front page had a photograph of both him and Savannah with a heading which stated. 'Returning Home?' Damian was not happy about the question mark. He was now more concerned for Savannah.

The return journey for both Savannah and Damian allowed them to reflect on the past eight weeks. Some of it was joyous, others not so. Savannah reached Juba and was met by Mr Baldwin. He had already read the newspaper in Juba about Savannah returning home. He was quite angry about the story. Damian returned home to his wife Klara and daughter Suzanna to continue their life as best they could. They thanked God for enriching their lives with their daughter Savannah even for a precious little while.

Chapter 11

As days and months passed by, Savannah and the family learned more about each other from telephone calls, text messages and letters. They looked forward to the correspondence. A year on, slowly but surely they were becoming a family unit. Klara however felt that Savannah had distanced herself from her. Klara was not able to cope with life in general. Throughout the years she continued with counselling sessions but with not much progress. She became an introvert and spoke very little with Damian. She believed that it was her negligence that contributed to losing her daughter. She consulted the best specialists but gradually she became weak. Suzanna gave immense support when she was at home but feared the worst. One morning when Suzanna brought Klara's breakfast to bed she found her dead. Beside her was an empty bottle of prescribed medication. Damian was informed at the university. He was heart broken. He immediately informed Savannah and she arranged to come for the funeral. Her attendance at the funeral was appreciated by both Damian and Suzanna. She was indeed of great support to them both. One day Savannah commented "mum has been so unlucky since we were born, she did not deserve the unhappiness."

After a months stay in England Savannah left for Juba. Damian and Suzanna carried on their lives as best they could, giving comfort and support to each other. Damian decided that he would retire from work and try some volunteering with 'Save the children.' He missed Klara and Savannah and looked forward to Suzanna returning from her flights.

During the next year Suzanna was dating her childhood friend Paul. He supported her as well as Damian. He fitted in well with their way of life and Damian got on well with him. Paul was a solicitor with a firm of lawyers in Manchester and enjoyed his work immensely. In November of that year Suzanna and Paul got married in church with a reception for friends and close relatives in a local hotel. Unfortunately Savannah could not attend the wedding owing to Martha Baldwin's illness. Although Suzanna was disappointed she respected Savannah's wishes. For their honeymoon they travelled to Seychelles. They brought back holiday pictures of them which were the envy of her friends. Suzanna posted the photographs to Savannah. She was excited and pleased for Suzanna and Paul.

Damian suggested to Suzanna and Paul "It would save both of you a lot of money if you would make your family home in Chipping." He continued "the house is too big for me to live alone, in any case I have written it for you Suzanna." Paul in Particular liked the house located in Chipping very much and so they started their marriage life there. Suzanna was in away glad that she could have an eye on Damian. In general Damian, Suzanna and Paul were comfortable with each other's company.

Exactly six months following Suzanna and Paul's wedding the three of them were into their evening meal when the land phone rang. Damian said "let us not be disturbed during our meal." The caller can leave a message." There was a message and it was from Philip. The message said "Mr Damian I think you will remember me. Please call me on this number. It is urgent." Damian commented "Why does he want to contact me after all these years I wonder?" Damian said "Philip is always trouble." Suzanna said "You might as well call him, dad" once you finish your meal." When Damian did call Philip he said, "Mr Damian, I have bad news for you, your daughter in Juba has met with an accident. Jerome just called. The embassy would know more about it." He then ended the call. Damian was speechless and he went pale. He said "Its Savannah." Suzanna said "what about her?" Damian shook his head and muttered "She has met with an accident" and collapsed onto the chair next to him. Suzanna said, "Paul can get the British Embassy." He then dialled the number and gave it to Suzanna when it started to ring. Paul quickly got some water and attended to Damian. The voice said "This is the on-call service of the Consulate-General in Cape Town, how can I help you?" Suzanna replied "I am calling on behalf of Mr Damian Sinclair in England. We believe his daughter Savannah has met with an accident in Juba. Please could you let us know the facts?" The voice replied "we don't generally get such information here in South Africa however, since we know Mr Sinclair we can find out and call you back" Suzanna gave the number and closed the call.

Suzanna made a cup of tea for the three of them. Meanwhile Damian felt better. These were anxious moments for all but it was a long wait. At around 21.00 hours the phone rang again. This time Damian wanted to answer the call. Suzanna sat him on the armchair prior to answering it. He heard Mr Fenton's voice. He said "Mr Sinclair, I am sorry it took so long, the news is not good. I had to get in touch with the embassy in Khartoum. Your daughter and one of her colleagues were on a field trip to a remote part of Juba. On their return, their Land Rover had been ambushed. Your daughter and her colleague have been shot and killed. The bodies have been found on the roadside by the police. I am so very sorry Mr Sinclair. Mr and Mrs Baldwin have been informed." At this Damian just did not want to know more. Suzanna took the receiver and said "Mr Fenton this is Suzanna I will arrange a flight for us to be in Juba right away." Mr Fenton commented "we will try to get more information and assist you in whatever way we can."

Suzanna was in shock but she had to support her dad and do the necessary actions as fast as possible. She called her grandparents on both sides. They were distraught. She then called the Foreign office and asked them to help with obtaining emergency visas for the three of them. She called British Airways reservations to obtain three return tickets to Juba. Damian finally spoke with Mr Baldwin and informed him of their arrival in Juba. It took one whole day to obtain the necessary documents and they left for Juba within 48 hours on a B.A. flight. The pilot and the cabin crew were very understanding and expressed their sympathy which was appreciated by the family.

After a very long journey they changed flight at Cape Town for Juba. On their arrival at the Juba airport they were met by Mr Baldwin. He looked pale and forlorn. They shook hands with each other. He said "Martha, my wife is ill in bed. The sad news has not helped her." Mr Baldwin continued "I have arranged the UNCHR guest house for you. The hotels are expensive. I will escort you there."

Mr Baldwin said "Savannah was a methodical girl. She wrote the instructions should she die. Here it is. Accordingly she wanted to be cremated in Juba and her ashes to be scattered in the Blue Nile which she adored. We will honour her last wish." He commented "Savannah was too good for this world. She had to go. We have given all our love, the best way we can. She deserved the very best. I am so glad she made the trip to England." On her return we discussed many issues which were dear to her heart. She was very mature for her age and took her responsibilities seriously. Her work colleagues will surely miss her." Damian, Suzanna and Paul listened to Mr Baldwin. They were still in shock and had no words to describe their sadness.

The police investigations were slow. The Police department were not happy for the family to have a viewing of Savannah before they completed their immediate investigations. Their response indicated "This was an unprovoked attack by more than one person. We still don't know who did it."

In the meantime friends, colleagues and well wishes came to meet them and express their sympathy. The UNCHR office was to give a day of mourning for Savannah's colleagues on the day of the funeral.

After a week in Juba, the family was allowed to see the body of Savannah. They could not recognise her at all. This was too much for Damian who was sobbing. Suzanna had to be brave for her dad's sake. Paul was glad that he accompanied them to give his support in this time of sadness.

Mr Baldwin and his colleagues arranged the funeral, cremation. The date of the funeral was notified in the local newspapers. Martha Baldwin was too ill to travel. Damian, Suzanna, Paul, several friends, colleagues and well wishers were present to see her ashes scattered in the Blue Nile according to Savannah's wishes.

Mr Baldwin discussed that Savannah was concerned about the newspaper articles and journalists taking photographs of her. She had informed Mrs Baldwin that at times there were men who stalked her all day. "When I reported these incidents to the police they did not want to know. That's how good our police department is. Fear not I will keep pushing to know who the perpetrators are. I will let you know."

On their return journey Damian, Suzanna and Paul took a flight to Cape Town. They met with Mr Fenton and Mr Barrington-Hines to express their thanks for all the work done on the family's behalf. They did appreciate the gesture although the accident happened in Sudan. Having broken their journey for three hours they took a B.A. flight to Manchester. They arrived in Manchester in the early hours of the morning. Damian and Suzanna looked as they had aged in just two weeks. After having rested for a few days they were ready to face family and friends.

Suzanna supported Damian in every way possible. She realised her enormous responsibility for the future. Damian tried hard to cope with daily life, but having lost his wife Klara and daughter Savannah he gave up hope and the will to live. He had no strength to carry on. The continued tragic life events were too much for him. He felt helpless and hopeless. Eight months after Savannah was killed Damian passed away in his sleep of natural causes. Suzanna informed Mr Fenton of her dad's death for the records. She also spoke of the tragedy with Mr Baldwin.

After seven months had passed Mr Fenton sent a letter to Suzanna and enclosed a letter from the police department in Juba. This stated:

"Detail investigation of the murder has taken place but up to now we were unable to convict the murderer/s owing to the absence of reliable evidence." The case is on our books until such time further evidence comes to light."

It was left for Suzanna to explain in time to her children, the horrendous story of her parents' and sister's lives which started full of promise but ended in disaster after disaster. A "Newswire" having interfered with the happiness of one generation, spilled over to the next generation, because of greed for other people's money.

*"For Evil to flourish all that is needed
Is for good people to do nothing."*

Edmund Burke

Acknowledgements

To my friends Brenda Lavender, Margaret Fagan, Ruth Grimley, Eileen Banister, Joan Stott, Jackie Griffihs, Judith Ball and Paul Hickman for their continued support.

To Jackie Griffiths for her art work on the front and back cover of this book.

For the British Telecom Tech Experts for their support and skill.

For Venus Taylor, the design consultant and her team at Authorhouse for their continued support and skill.

About the Author

Dr Ummanga Jolly (nee Lankatilleke) was born in Sri Lanka. She came to England in 1961. She holds a PhD from the University of Durham, LLB (Hons) from the Open University, a Master in Education and a Bachelor in Education (Hons) from the Victoria University of Manchester along with Registered Nurse, Midwifery, and Teaching Certificates.

She has travelled extensively around the world and has a wide interest in writing and photography. She devotes her leisure time to her pet cats and is a cricket enthusiast.

Her recent publications are "Before I forget my life" and "Little things that touched my heart published by Authorhouse.

She presently lives in the leafy Brockhall Village in the heart of Lancashire England.

Printed in Great Britain
by Amazon.co.uk, Ltd.,
Marston Gate.